MAO vs. CHIANG
The Battle for China,
1925–1949

MAO vs. CHIANG
The Battle for China,
1925—1949

A THISTLE BOOK

Published by

GROSSET & DUNLAP, INC.

A National General Company

New York

Library of Congress Catalog Card No. 75-86716
ISBN: 0-448-21437-7 (trade edition)
ISBN: 0-448-26204-5 (library edition)

Printed in the United States of America

FOR VICTORIA AND SIMON
who were born there—
and their millions of contemporaries
Chinese and American

Contents

CHAPTER 1

"The Revolution Is Not Yet Completed"

THE GRAY-HAIRED man who lay ill in a walled house in the Tatar City of Peking was not yet fifty-nine, but his bluff cheeks were sunken and the determined mouth under his bristling mustache was twisted with pain. Dr. Sun Yat-sen, who had briefly been the president of the newly established Republic of China in 1912, was dying of cancer in the early spring of 1925. His lifework was far from done. He had not succeeded in creating a united, forward-looking nation under the rule of parliamentary democracy, adapted to traditional Chinese forms of government.

He had been a legend in his own adventurous lifetime. Now he was being transformed into a semi-mythical hero of a new nationalist cult even before his death. Although the American doctors of the Peking Union Medical College had found the cancer inoperable, still practitioners of traditional Chinese herbal medicine and acupuncture came and went, applying their own ancient remedies.

But the politicians who thronged about Sun Yat-sen's bed knew that their leader was dying. Despite the love some of them bore him, they were chiefly concerned with exploiting the cult they had created for immediate political purposes, rather than for the man himself. All looked first to advancing themselves and their policies; all excepting, of course, his son and his wife, Soong Ching-ling, daughter of one of the wealthiest and most Western-oriented families of China.

Dr. Sun Yat-sen was the first major Chinese political leader who possessed true understanding of the outside world. It was, therefore, fitting that foreign friends and advisers were prominent among the watchers at his bedside. The representative of the Communist International (Comintern), Michael Borodin, had as great an interest as the Chinese politicians in exploiting the legend that would spring up around the dying leader. Chief among the Chinese was Wang Ching-wei, who had drawn up Sun Yat-sen's political testament. The brief document stressed one commanding sentence: "At present, the revolution is not yet completed." That sentence was to describe—and dominate—the country's political life for the next two and a half decades, as China sought a new identity and new relationships with herself and with the intrusive Western world.

Two men, both members of Dr. Sun Yat-sen's Kuomintang, the Chinese National People's Party, were absent from Peking while their leader lay dying. One was a young Japanese-trained army officer called Chiang Kai-shek, who would win the first great victory and become president of the Republic of China. The other man was a few years younger, a scrappily educated agitator from central Hunan Province named Mao Tse-tung, who had been a founding member of the Communist Party of China in 1921. He was to rally the discontented peasants and, almost a quarter of a century later, become Chairman of the Communist People's Republic of China, after driving his rival, Chiang, into exile. Between the millstones of their antagonism, both personal and political, these temporary allies of 1925 were to grind the Chinese people and create a seemingly perpetual state of war and chaos.

The death of Dr. Sun marked the beginning, rather than the end of an era, for he was a man far in advance of his time. His multitude of pseudonyms demonstrated the ups and downs of his career. Known to the West by his original name, Sun Yat-set, he was called by the Chinese either Sun Wen, the name he himself preferred and signed to his political testament, or Sun Chung-shan, the alias he had used for concealment when he fled to political exile in Japan. The man who, like Moses, died viewing the promised land he would never enter, had used many other aliases. They have been largely forgotten, for they were put on and off like worn-out coats. They were necessary since Dr. Sun had chiefly worked abroad to make a revolution in China. He had not chosen that sphere voluntarily, but had been forced into exile by the Manchu Dynasty, whose agents still pursued him while he raised financial support among Chinese living abroad. He had first come to worldwide attention when he was rescued from illegal imprisonment in the Imperial Chinese Embassy in London.

The man who today is honored by both Nationalists and Communists as the father of modern China actually spent more of his fifty-nine years abroad than in his native country. He attended high school in Honolulu and medical school in the British Crown Colony of Hong Kong. Afterwards, he wandered across the globe seeking diplomatic and military support from foreign powers, as well as recruits and funds from Chinese colonies overseas, in his campaign to destroy the decadent Manchu Empire and replace it with a "modern" government. After his first revolution had failed, he finally obtained the powerful backing he required from the newly born Soviet Union. But his own vision of the future of China was made up almost equally of Western democratic and traditional Chinese ingredients—later seasoned with Soviet authoritarianism.

By the early 1920s, the Kuomintang, the Nationalist Party, had been reorganized into a tightly disciplined, semi-totalitarian organization on the Communist model by Dr. Sun's Soviet advisers, who also helped train his armies. But the administration he envisioned for China embodied the checks and balances of the Western parliamentary tradition. Instead of three branches, as in the West, there were, however, to be five: the normal executive, legislature, and judiciary with co-equal Examination and Censorate Councils. The Chinese had, after all, invented the Civil Service Examination System, while the Censors of the Empire, like the Roman Tribunes, had been charged to call attention to inefficiency and corruption in the other branches—much as the Inspector-General of the U.S. Army does. That political structure, combined with moderate Socialism, might well have worked. The tragedy was that it was never given an honest trial— as much because of men's perversity as because of unfortunate circumstances.

The unique scheme of government had grown directly from Dr. Sun's own experiences. He embodied in himself the conflict between Chinese and Western values, customs, techniques and systems, which had dominated the history of China since insistent Westerners had arrived in force in the early 1800s. They had demanded trade and diplomatic relations on equal terms with the all-powerful Empire, which could not grant equality without denying its basic principle of Chinese superiority. That conflict is still unresolved, and it still dominates the political life of China.

Sun was not only the first Chinese leader who knew the West at first hand. He was also the first to receive a thorough Western education, as well as a traditional Chinese education in the Confucian Classics. Those classical writings, exalted by Confucius in the 6th Century B.C., were not only the basis of all knowledge of the old China but the foundation of her political and ethical systems. Some of Dr. Sun's critics declared that his Chinese education was inferior to his Western learning. He hardly bothered to deny the charge, for his mere possession of a Western medical degree made him all but unique in the closing days of the 19th Century, when the enfeebled Empire still ruled China. Instead, the man from the restless south devoted all his energies to overthrowing the Confucian moral and political systems. He believed that the petrified customs and organizations, originally formed more than 2,000 years earlier, were the greatest obstacles to attaining his goals, expressed in his chief work, *The Three People's Principles.*

Those principles, laboriously evolved by the dedicated political leader after much reading and consultation, can be expressed simply, though their origins were complex.

Chief among them was the Principle of Nationalism, which—by intent, rather than by chance—was expressed by a term that means in Chinese "racialism," as well as "nationalism." Dr. Sun felt that the Chinese race and the Chinese nation were inseparable. He grieved that they had been humiliated and exploited by the superior material force of the West after a series of one-sided wars. His overriding purpose was to restore China to the position of respect and power she had enjoyed in the world she had known before the Westerners arrived. The rest of the world, he declared, was devouring China, carving up her territory and her rights slice by slice.

Next in importance ranked the Principle of the People's Power. Dr. Sun did not envision perfect democracy such as the West has always sought but never attained. He believed that his people were not prepared for complete self-rule, and he proposed, instead, the elaborate system of checks and balances of his five-part governmental system. After a "period of tutelage," full democracy would, he suggested, be instituted by stages.

Last was the Principle of the People's Welfare, the least systematized—and for the moment—the least important of the Three Principles. Dr. Sun had put together an outline of an economic system which would, he hoped, level the great differences between rich and poor in a vast country which was industrially backward, but rich in natural resources. His plan foresaw not only the economic development of China toward modern industrialization, a necessity for the realization of the Principle of Nationalism, but reform of the archaic system of land ownership, which kept the Chinese farmer permanently poor. Demonstrating the breadth of Dr. Sun's interests, his last principle also provided for urban land reform, which would, through selective taxes, insure that land in the cities was also devoted to the public good.

But he was a long way from realizing those ideal plans when, in March, 1925, he lay dying in the bedroom that looked out on a walled courtyard in Peking. After the Revolution in 1911 destroyed the Empire, Dr. Sun had served briefly as president of the newly established Republic of China. He had seen his dreams crushed by the insatiable ambitions of the military leaders who actually controlled the country piecemeal. He had resigned the presidency, hoping to bring unity to the nation, but his sacrifice had intensified the chaos. The sentence, at once bitter and commanding, in his political testament, reflected his profound frustration: "The revolution is not yet completed!"

The revolution *should* have been completed by 1925, and the nation *should* have seen the beginning of the ordered prosperity Dr. Sun had envisioned. China should also have been moving toward the universal international respect for her new power which was his most important purpose. He had himself worked for many years to prepare the Revolution of 1911, which finally destroyed the last dynasty of the Chinese Empire, a dynasty already weakened by a century of civil revolt and intermittent war with the greedy "Western barbarians." But neither his prodigious efforts nor his self-sacrificing surrender of the presidency had served to create the new nation Dr. Sun sought. He was more a visionary than a practical politician. Circumstances and men's greed had both played him false. The revolution was not yet completed. In truth, it had hardly begun.

The Revolution of 1911, ignited by the premature blast of an agitator's bomb, had been nearly bloodless, because the Empire had actually fallen of its own weight, like a great wooden building so eaten by dryrot and termites that it collapses under a puff of wind. But the idealists surrounding Dr. Sun possessed neither the organization nor the resources to build a new structure on the ruins. Instead, ambitious realists staked out their own claims by military power. They were known to the West as warlords. In 1915, Yüan Shi-k'ai, the greatest warlord, died. He was the man who had become president of the Republic of China after Sun Yat-sen resigned, and he had attempted to make himself Emperor. Shifting alliances of smaller warlords dominated the country for the next decade. The glorious revolution had produced not a new China, but political chaos.

For convenience, foreign powers dealt with the warlord who happened to hold the ancient capital of Peking,
adjusting their diplomatic recognition of the "legitimate" government as new warlords conquered the Imperial City. For profit, foreigners offered support to their
favorite warlords, in return for economic concessions.
Instead of creating a proud and independent China, the
glorious Revolution had made China even more vulnerable to the depredations of the West.

Dr. Sun had gone into exile, first in Japan, and later in
the International Settlement of Shanghai, where he was
given the sanctuary the foreign administration had always offered Chinese political fugitives. He finally began
to build his own power base in his own native area, the
southern metropolis of Canton, 90 miles from British
Hong Kong. By the early 1920s, he had secured the
support of the Soviet Union and the Communist International. He was granted diplomatic recognition, can-
cellation of the "unequal treaties" the West had used to
exploit China, and the military, economic, and political
assistance he needed to build his strength. His purpose
remained constant. He was determined to drive the warlords from power and to unite China under his own
half-democratic Republic.

Despite his wide general reading, Dr. Sun was primarily a political man. Culture, as such, interested him
only if it would serve his political ends. But while he
struggled to fulfill his political dreams, there were
strange stirrings in the world of literature. Though literature and politics may appear quite far apart, those stirrings were to exert an influence on the development of
modern China as great as Dr. Sun's political activities.

In China, literature, in the broadest sense, had always
been inseparable from politics—and morals. The Chinese Empire had been ruled for more than two thousand

years by a group of scholar-officials, qualified for their positions by passing civil service examinations based on the classical Confucian literature. It had not been a bad way of insuring a uniform level of education and understanding among officials ruling a vast and diverse land.

But, about 1917, young men began to do something about the century-old complaint that the study of the Confucian Classics produced a hidebound, unimaginative bureaucracy which was instinctively resistant to the political, technical, and moral innovations essential to making China a modern nation that could compete in the industrial world. A classical scholar with modern ideas, named Ch'en Tu-hsiu, began publishing a magazine called *The New Youth*, which became a platform not only for new ideas, but also for proposals for reforming the code-like style of all Chinese writing, really a separate language from the spoken language. It was essential to alter the nature of government, as well as the way men thought—and the basis of government was the classical language. Ch'en therefore contended that it was equally essential to create a new style of writing.

The new style, called *pai-hua*, meaning "plain language," was adopted by only a handful of writers. But their inspiration moved university students to re-examine the nature of both education and the government of the country. The students, always a privileged class because of traditional Chinese reverence for learning, finally burst forth in political action on May 4th, 1919. Rioting against the warlord government's acceptance of twenty-one Japanese demands—which would have reduced China to a colony—they forced the government to retract. A new force had appeared in Chinese politics—popular demonstrations led by students.

The universities of Peking had also become centers of study of the new doctrine of Marxism, which had just triumphed in Russia. Beginning with study clubs, students and professors soon moved on to political activity, and in July, 1921, the Communist Party of China was founded. Ch'en was its first Secretary-General.

The warlords were still dominant throughout the nation—and particularly in Peking. But Dr. Sun's Nationalist Party, the Kuomintang, and the Communists both had strong ties to Moscow. Both sides reluctantly agreed to a limited alliance. The few thousand Communists would be allowed to join the Nationalist Party as *individuals*, while remaining members of the Communist Party. It was thus that Mao-Tse-tung became an important member of the Shanghai Committee of the Kuomintang, while Ch'en was raised to the Nationalist Party's Central Executive Committee. Although neither side really desired the alliance, both were forced by Moscow to agree to pool their strength for the moment. The Communists, however, were promised that the Nationalists would be used to destroy the warlords and then be "cast aside like a squeezed lemon."

The relationship was uneasy. Different personalities, different political purposes, and different personal ambitions divided the Nationalists and the Communists. Moreover, most Soviet military, technical, and economic aid was going to the Nationalist forces in the south around Canton. There, Dr. Sun, claiming his rights as elected president of the Republic of China, had established his government and his general headquarters as military Commander-in-Chief. Nonetheless, the Communists proved most useful in agitating among the peasants, the students, and the small laboring class. When the Whampoa Military Academy was established in Canton in May, 1924, its faculty was mixed. Michael Borodin, the Comintern (Communist International) representative, was appointed political adviser; the young General

Chiang Kai-shek was made Commandant; and the chief Political Commissar, appointed in accordance with the Russian system, was a young man named Chou En-lai, recently returned from France, where he had organized the first overseas branch of the Chinese Communist Party.

The Nationalist-Communist alliance was preparing for war as the only means of destroying the warlords. Though there was strain within the alliance, a powerful faction in the Kuomintang found that, for the moment, its interests ran closer to the Communists' interests than to those of the conservatives within the Nationalist Party. Even Chiang became an honorary member of the Central Executive Committee of the Communist International—and was denounced as a "Red brigand" by foreign powers and foreign businessmen. The two essentially antagonistic parties remained bound by common interests—for the moment.

Although the alliance was building a modern military machine to sweep the warlords from China by force, Dr. Sun was still negotiating with some warlords in the hope of winning them to his side—and splitting the warlord alliance which held Peking. In November, 1924, he set out on his last journey. He went to Peking to confer with the warlord government. His fatal illness overtook him while he was in Peking—and sharply altered the course of the incomplete revolution.

But the events he had set in motion continued to move forward. Chinese youths and laborers, protesting against British rule, were shot by British troops in Shanghai on May 30th, 1925, and a protest movement began. That movement ended in a great general strike which tied up Hong Kong and Canton, giving the Communists the opportunity to vastly enlarge their power among the working class. A man named Liu Shao-ch'i, later to be president of the Communist People's Republic of China, became vice-chairman of the leftist All-China Labor Federation. Communist power attained a rate of rapid expansion it was not to enjoy again for a decade.

At the same time, Chiang's armies, composed of both Communists and Nationalists, cleared the last remaining warlord troops from the area around the Nationalist base in Canton. Earlier, Wang Ching-wei, Dr. Sun's spiritual heir, had been elected chairman of the Central Executive Committee of the Kuomintang. The Nationalists, it appeared, had set their organization in order for the march north. Wang, the civilian, was the chief political leader, while military responsibility rested with General Chiang. The Nationalists, further, appeared to have established a firm working alliance with the Communists. The force that would destroy warlord rule was truly almost complete. But conflicting interests within that force actually prepared the way for even greater strife.

CHAPTER 2

To the North

ALTHOUGH RELATIONS WERE tense and the alliance was already threatened, it still worked. The Ko-ming Chün, the Revolutionary Army, under the command of Generalissimo Chiang Kai-shek, with General Chou En-lai its chief political commissar, was—both politically and in outward appearance—a unique new force in China when it marched out of Canton on June 6th, 1926. After a century of grudging changes toward Western ways China had, for the first time, fielded a modern army under modern discipline and armed with modern weapons, all attained chiefly through Soviet advice and Soviet aid. The troops were well clothed, and they carried their new rifles and machine guns with pride. The Revolutionary Army was composed of disparate units, ranging from its core of divisions personally recruited by Generalissimo Chiang and personally loyal to him, all the way to the troops of warlords who had subordinated their personal ambitions to the cause of unification. It was, nonetheless, greatly superior in every respect to the badly organized, ill-disciplined, and divided warlord forces against which it marched. The Northern Expedition, as the Nationalist forces called the campaign, was a holy crusade, animated by the spirit of the canonized Sun Yat-sen.

Even more important than the normal screen of scouts maneuvering ahead of the main body were the propagandists and agitators, open and secret, who smoothed the political path for the Revolutionary Army. Chiefly made up of Communist-inclined "intellectuals," the propaganda units came under the direct control of Chou. Some operated just a few miles in front of the advancing armies. Other units might be hundreds of miles ahead, subverting the warlord troops and arousing the populace. Still other units were hundreds of miles behind, consolidating the victory in areas the troops had overrun and left. The rapid victories the Revolutionary Army began winning in the summer of 1926 were due almost as much to the "political work" of the Communist-directed units as to force of arms.

Besides, the Army's strikingly efficient appearance was a weapon as effective as either shots or words. Idealists and realists alike were awed by the mere fact that China had, finally, produced an army which looked equal to foreign forces. The Chinese had suffered too long from humiliations imposed by foreign powers with superior military machines not to rejoice proudly in possessing a comparable force at last, a force sworn to end exploitation and avenge humiliation. Besides, it was only prudent to yield to an army which appeared so overwhelmingly superior. Many Chinese battles had, for centuries, been decided before their onset by conceding victory to the side which presented a ferocious image of unquestionable superiority.

The propaganda units were a force as new and as potent as modern military techniques. They preached doctrines and made promises the people of China had rarely heard—the natural equality of all men and the necessity to destroy the "exploiting classes" before all men could enjoy economic and legal equality. A major theme of their message was, however, ancient. It had resounded across the countryside each time a dynasty fell—and dozens of dynasties had ruled within the classical tradition. "Land to the tiller!" the propagandists promised, echoing the promises of redistribution of wealth which had rallied the oppressed to the revolutionary cause throughout the ages. Dr. Sun's Principle of the People's Welfare was in the service of his Principle of Nationalism, though it was manipulated by the Communists and their sympathizers. It did not matter that Dr. Sun had himself flatly rejected Communism for China.

A typical member of the political units was Kuo Mojo, a poet who had taken a medical degree and later turned to politics. Kuo, who would later become a vice-premier of the Communist People's Republic, was chief of the Propaganda Unit of the Political Bureau of the Revolutionary Army. After conferring with Mao at the Canton home of another prominent Communist leader on June 24th, 1926, he marched out on the Northern Expedition. He got as far north as Wuhan, the triplet industrial cities of Central China, which were a major center of Communist strength in the labor movement, before concluding that soldiering was not really to his taste.

His pen was ready enough with joyous odes to the revolution and his own role in the revolution, unashamedly celebrating himself and his comrades as "heroes on horseback." But Kuo was really quite uncomfortable in the saddle of the elderly white horse of uncertain ancestry and disposition to which his rank entitled him. Despite its inexperienced rider's exhortations, Kuo's mount had formed one unalterable habit. Perhaps because it was a *Chinese* horse, it had learned, as had most Chinese, that it was safest to be in the middle, neither first nor last in the political movements which had cast the country into turmoil for three decades. Each morning, Kuo's horse would take a position just behind the mount of the chief of the Political Bureau—and would maintain that position throughout the day's journey. Both the Chinese chief and his Russian adviser were old cavalrymen, exuberant at finding themselves once again in the saddle after confinement in offices. In high spirits, they would urge their horses to the gallop, and Kuo's old white horse would follow, faithful to his training. After bouncing uncomfortably across the rough countryside for three days, the poet decided to make an altruistic gesture. He was, he said, willing to walk and allow his horse to carry the baggage of the company.

Wuhan was taken that summer, almost without a fight, and the National Revolutionary Army found itself halfway to its goal of Peking. Kuo reverted with a sigh of relief to administrative work behind a desk in a chair that was, providentially, not given to uncontrollable gallops across the countryside. But he was soon dismayed by new and more acute distress. The quarrel between the Nationalists and the Communists, with whom he was allied, was becoming intense. When he protested that the provisional government established in Wuhan was following policies which betrayed the spirit of the revolution, he was soothed with promises and explanations. Certain compromises were necessary, he was told, but they were merely "tactical." Such "temporary" measures would be corrected when the revolution had achieved total victory by taking Peking and destroying the power of the warlords, thus unifying the nation.

But the idealistic young poet finally became disgusted with the course of politics. He denounced the crusading revolution as a monster, "a sheep's head on a dog's body," in obvious reference to the incongruous alliance of Nationalists and Communists. In 1927, he retreated to Shanghai, having discovered that it was one thing to write odes to the revolution and quite another to endure the physical and mental discomforts of participating in a revolution.

Many curious events occurred between the conquest of Wuhan and Kuo's break with the confused revolution. Key roles were played by graduates of the Whampoa Military Academy, established in 1924 on the advice of Sun's Soviet advisers. Although Whampoa had graduated no more than a few thousand officers, they were the hard core of the Revolutionary Army. Not only Chiang's modern, central units were staffed by Whampoa graduates, but even allied divisions were liberally seeded with their classmates. Despite its brief life, Whampoa already had developed an "image" and a tradition comparable to West Point or Sandhurst. Many officers became Communists under Chou's political tutelage; others rejected the alien doctrine in favor of the Three People's Principles of Dr. Sun and personal loyalty to Generalissimo Chiang. Regardless of their loyalties, they were key men, the only group of Chinese officers who had received systematic, modern military training. Whampoa became as much a symbol as a school.

Like the political commissar system, the officers' academy had been originated by Comintern advisers. They were the political agitator, Michael Borodin, Sun's closest foreign associate, who still retained much power; and the man known as General Galen, who, later, as Marshal Vasili Blyukher, commanded the Soviet Army of the Far East. Despite the strain between Nationalists and Communists, the system worked. The unification of China was being accomplished rapidly, though the forces that performed the feat were themselves hardly united.

The Wuhan cities were taken in the summer of 1926, and the Provisional National Government was established in Hankow, the chief of those cities. In November, 1926, warlord resistance began to evaporate. The Revolutionary Army took Shanghai, the chief metropolis of China, on March 22nd, 1927—and, a few days later, occupied Nanking, the traditional "southern capital" of the nation. Effective resistance was disappearing under the three-fold impact of guns, political agitation, and secret intrigue.

Peking lay ahead—and the road to Peking was open. It appeared that the revolution would shortly be completed with the unification of China under a strong central government. Dr. Sun Yat-sen's dream appeared on the verge of realization—a single government for a united nation —a government which would rule according to his Three People's Principles and make China once more strong, respected, and prosperous.

It had been almost too easy. Once the Revolutionary Army marched out of Canton and the political units began swarming across the countryside, the vaunted power of the warlords had nearly disintegrated.

The poorly paid, ill-fed, and uninspired troops of the warlords were half bandits and half soldiers, half volunteers and half conscripted by undiscriminating press gangs. Many had been driven into the predatory armies by the traditional pressures which had made bandits—or soldiers—of Chinese peasants for centuries.

Whenever disorder, deprivation, and disease stalked

the land, the exactions of tax collectors and officials became extreme. The poor peasant, unable to meet those demands, had no choice but to join the army or join the masterless men of the hills and swamps whom the authorities called brigands. Their lot was little better than it would have been had they remained in their impoverished villages, and their families were still exposed to starvation and exploitation. The soldiers did not think of themselves as heroes. They were, in 1927, as they had been in 527, little more than human cattle with guns, bound by poverty and fear to the ambition of their strutting and avaricious generals.

Pitted against a reasonably well-disciplined and well-armed regular force motivated by a unifying *esprit de corps*, the crusaders of the Revolutionary Army certainly would not have done so well. Even small, well-armed units could have held up their Blitzkrieg-like advance across the plains of central China. But the warlord armies had neither the will nor the means to resist their attacks. The troops of Wu P'ei-fu, one of the most feared of the so-called Northern Warlords, who had once held Peking itself, were driven north into Honan Province, on the edge of the home province of Hopei, where the capital itself lay. Wu's retreat from Wuhan had enabled Chiang to take the key industrial-and-communications complex without a fight. Wang, the political heir of Dr. Sun Yat-sen, thereupon established his provisional government in Hankow. Wu's armies had simply melted away.

The conquest of Shanghai in March, 1927, was almost equally easy, though the chief port of China had been held by the forces of General Sun Ch'üan-fang, who was considered invincible. The 118th Division of the Revolutionary Army had not even entered the great city on the mudflats of the Yangtze River Delta before Shanghai was theirs. Chiang had learned much from the Communists with whom he was still in uneasy alliance. He also understood the Chinese tradition well, and he knew that there were other—and, perhaps, better—ways of taking a city than laying a formal siege. After his consultations with the Chinese bankers and merchants of Shanghai, and after his promises to the foreign community, Shanghai fell into his hands without a fight. Sun Ch'üan-fang's hold over coastal Kiangsu and Chekiang Provinces was broken without a frontal engagement.

Nanking, the traditional southern capital of the Imperial Court, was the next target. The city which, second only to Peking, was the symbol of control over China, lay only 200 miles from Shanghai. The conquest of Nanking was to prove more difficult, if only marginally.

The Revolutionary Army had already had its first difficulties with the foreign powers in Shanghai, despite Chiang's clever diplomacy. The Nationalists were, after all, completing the revolution which was to make China independent, unified, and strong. Dr. Sun had stressed that they musy drive "foreign exploiters" from China or, at the very least, deprive the foreigners of their "extraterritorial" rights, the power to administer "foreign concessions" under foreign law. Inspired by that mission, the Revolutionary Army had pressed against the foreign concessions of Shanghai, a city almost entirely under foreign rule. They had been kept from occupying those concessions only by a strong show of foreign force. Prudent in victory, Chiang had drawn back on the verge of conflict with foreign troops. The time, he felt, was not ripe. Besides, a frontal assault was not necessarily the best way to drive out the foreigners, any more than it had been the best way to take Shanghai itself.

Chiang moved his troops rapidly out of Shanghai, hurrying to Nanking by railroad before stiffening resistance could prevent his completing the conquest of Kiangsu Province. The attitude of the foreigners was already changing. They were muttering that the Nationalists, and particularly Chiang himself, were nothing more than "Red brigands in alliance with the godless Communists." The latter had made no secret of their policies, which included the ultimate sin in the eyes of the Western commercial community: they had no respect for private property. Moreover, the warlords of the north, with whom Dr. Sun was negotiating when he died, were beginning to close ranks in awareness of their common peril. Tension was also rising between the Communists and their allies, the so-called left-wing Kuomintang, on the one hand, and, on the other, the conservative, right-wing forces centering around Chiang Kai-shek. The revolution was being completed, but the revolutionary forces were splintering.

Because of those pressures, Chiang moved against Nanking, the old walled city on the Yangtze River, even before he had consolidated his hold on Shanghai. For the first time, the Revolutionary Army ran into serious resistance. Though Nanking offered but a harassing defense, the passions of the troops were aroused. They escaped the effective control of their leaders, and they looted and killed for several days. Foreigners were a special target, though subsequent accounts of the carnage wreaked undoubtedly have been exaggerated. It was, however, not only the killing, which sent foreigners and rich Chinese fleeing to refuge, that provoked the first foreign intervention against the Revolutionary Army. The truly provocative deed was setting fire to the large storage tanks of foreign oil companies.

By the garish light of the burning oil tanks, British and American gunboats of the Yangtze River Patrol converged on the city. Their guns were small, but their aim

was good—and the Chinese were still swayed by unrea-
soning fear of Western military supremacy. A few bar-
rages from the gunboats ended the looting and restored
discipline to the Revolutionary Army. But the break between the Nationalists and their new foreign supporters
had become marked. It would require much effort to
restore friendly relations—and the cost would be high.

The Nanking incident also greatly stiffened the resistance of the Northern Warlords. They were still holding
the two northernmost provinces of China proper, Honan
and Hopei, as well as the Manchurian redoubt of Marshal Chang beyond the Great Wall. As a result of internal
dissension and external resistance, more than a year
passed between the capture of Nanking in March, 1927,
and the final campaign against the most important target
in China, the cultural and political center of Peking,
where the foreign diplomatic colony resided.

Chiang Kai-shek was finally ready to move against Peking in the spring of 1928. Once again, he employed his
familiar tactics of intrigue and political maneuvering,
backed by a show of military force. Though the Kuomintang's right wing, Chiang's chief support, was totally
alienated from the Communists by 1928, he had learned
Communist tactics well. Once again, he outflanked a key
position politically, rather than assaulting it directly.
Chiang entered into negotiations with Feng Yü-hsiang,
the so-called Christian General, an enormous man with
tremendously powerful hands and a domed head that
looked as big as a watermelon, who baptized his troops
with firehoses. The second leg of the triumvirate Chiang
formed with the warlords was the independent and
crochety Yen Hsi-shan, master of Shansi Province to the
west of Peking. Since Marshal Chang, the satrap of Manchuria, was isolated and later killed by a Japanese bomb,
Chiang finally took Peking in early June, 1928.

The Northern Expedition was completed after just two years. The country was, apparently, unified under a single central government for the first time since the early 19th Century. The final phase had been marred by clashes with Japanese troops illegally occupying the Shantung Peninsula, but the Japanese finally withdrew. Marshal Chang's son, the Young Marshal Chang Hsüeh-liang, who had succeeded to his father's power, could not formally bring Manchuria into the fold because of dominant Japanese influence there. But he swore allegiance and was given a senior position in the councils of the Nationalist Government.

Wang Ching-wei had fallen from power with his left-wing Kuomintang, while the Communists were totally disorganized. The seat of government was transferred to Nanking. Peking, the traditional center of government, was renamed Peiping. The new name meant Northern Peace; the old name meant Northern Capital. Chiang held all civil, as well as military, power in his hands, as chief of the government established in Nanking in October, 1928. The triumphant Nationalists seemed ready to put Dr. Sun's Three People's Principles into effect. It appeared that the revolution was finally completed and that Dr. Sun's spirit could rest in peace.

CHAPTER 3

The Shattered Alliance

VICTORY—OR EVEN the scent of victory—should have strengthened the alliance of the Nationalists and the Communists. Logically, the two parties making a successful revolution should have been bound together by the ties of mutual self-interest. It is, after all, normal to wait until power is won before squabbling over the spoils of victory. But normal logic did not operate. Strained even before the Northern Expedition began, the alliance broke some time before formal victory was attained by the capture of Peking and the proclamation of the new government.

The apparent logic of history did not operate in this case because of a number of special factors. The expectation that the two parties would have cooperated till their joint cause was won overlooked their peculiarly Chinese character and rivalries, as well as the indecisive Communist International in Moscow. The Comintern was, in any event, having its own difficulties. After the death in

1924 of V.I. Lenin, the Sun Yat-sen of the Russian revolution, the conflict between Leon Trotsky and Joseph Stalin became acute, bitter, and sanguinary. Inevitably, the "China Question" became a major element in the quarrel over policy and principle which only half masked a fierce struggle for personal power.

From the beginning, the most significant fact was that neither the Communists nor the Nationalists really wished to form an alliance to conquer China *together*. Both were compelled to do so by Moscow. The Comintern was convinced that a "national bourgeois" revolution must precede the "proletarian" revolution that would, finally, give power to the Communists. Behind the rigid Marxist formula, which took little account of actual conditions in China, lay a simple analysis, based on European history. Karl Marx, the father of the doctrine, had written that the bourgeoisie—that is, bankers, merchants, and small proprietors—must first "seize power" from the aristocracy before the succeeding—and final—revolution could give power into the hands of the "proletariat"—that is, the working class which owned nothing. As the "representative of the proletariat," the Communist Party would thus come to power—and only thus. In the judgment of the Comintern's members, the Kuomintang represented the bourgeoisie. They felt that the Communists' turn had not yet come.

Behind the confusing Marxist abstractions and the loud dedication to "humanitarian internationalism," the Soviet Union was pursuing its own *national* interests. With its longer history and greater numbers, its territorial base, and its military power, the Kuomintang looked much like the winner, while the infant Communist movement looked like a long shot. The Soviet leaders, naturally, preferred a winner. Besides, Marxism gave them a two-fold excuse for advancing immediate Russian national interests at the expense of the interests of international Communism. First, the Soviet Union *had* to be secure and powerful because it was the essential base, the "motherland of worldwide Communism." Second, the Chinese Communists could only gain power after the Nationalists had done so.

Despite their natural reluctance—and the suspicion they felt toward Moscow from the beginning—the Chinese Communists had little choice but to follow the Comintern's orders. In Canton as early as May, 1922, the first session of the Second National Congress of the Communist Party had agreed to "cooperate" with the Kuomintang in a "democratic revolution" which would be "anti-imperialist and anti-warlord." In July, 1922, the second session of the same Congress had convened on the shores of the blossom-embowered West Lake in the resort city of Hangchow. The Chinese Communist Party agreed to permit its members to enter the Kuomintang "as individuals."

Nonetheless, Ch'en Tu-hsiu, Secretary-General of the Party had revealed his misgivings. He tried to justify the burgeoning alliance to which he came so unwillingly by drawing a sharp distinction between those "national bourgeois elements" with whom the Communists might make common cause and other "bourgeois elements" who were the implacable enemy of the "proletariat" because they were allies of "foreign imperialism." Ch'en further stressed in his public writings that the alliance was a temporary measure, in effect good only until the "national bourgeois revolution" had been won. It was hardly the best way to win the confidence of the Kuomintang or to insure effective cooperation.

After the Communists had grudgingly submitted, Moscow sent a new representative to China. He was Adolf Joffe, and he was accredited to the government of

Sun Yat-sen, rather than the Communists. After much discussion, Sun and Joffe in January, 1923, issued a joint pronouncement which shocked the Chinese Communists. Conditions in China, the Soviet Union officially declared, were not suitable to Communism. The Soviet would, therefore, support the Nationalists.

The Communists' suspicions were confirmed. They feared, with good reason, that Moscow was more concerned with creating a Chinese government it could dominate than with the "victory of the working class." Nonetheless, the Communists went along—in word and deed. Despite their antagonism to the Russians, they had already submitted themselves to the discipline of the Comintern—and they could not retract that submission without tearing their own weak organization to pieces. They were learning the invaluable lesson that Moscow regarded Communist parties abroad as pawns to be moved—or sacrificed—for Moscow's interests.

In June, 1923, the Third National Congress of the Chinese Communist Party, meeting once again in the Nationalist stronghold of Canton, called upon all "social revolutionary elements to rally around the Kuomintang." The message was soon made more explicit by specific orders to students, peasant associations, and labor unions to support the Nationalist cause. The Communists had made their formal submission. But it was not until January of 1924 that the Kuomintang agreed to allow members of the Communist Party and its satellite, the Socialist Youth Corps, to join the Nationalist Party "as individuals."

The Communist Party still counted no more than four hundred members, while the Youth Corps' strength was approximately 4,000. Nonetheless, a Communist was raised to almost equal status with Dr. Sun in the Kuomintang, while Secretary-General Ch'en became a member of the Kuomintang's Central Executive Committee. Also, as has also been noted previously, lesser men like Mao Tse-tung were also given important posts.

The year 1924, notable also for the establishment of the Whampoa Military Academy, was the high point of Kuomintang-Chinese Communist Party cooperation. It was, by no coincidence, the first year of that cooperation. The reason for the Kuomintang's ready agreement to admit Communists was illuminated when Dr. Sun appointed the Comintern's representative, Michael Borodin, "Senior Adviser" to the Kuomintang in July, 1924. Borodin, after all, was not merely a source of advice, but, more important, the man who controlled the flow of guns and funds from Moscow. To seal the bargain, Sun sent Chiang to the Soviet Union on a "good will tour."

But open dissension between the two Chinese parties began soon after Dr. Sun's death in March, 1925. The Russians, it soon became apparent, were playing a double game, while the Chinese Communists made no secret of their strategy of using the Nationalists and then destroying them. If both Moscow's and the Chinese Communists' plans were somewhat ambitious in the light of reality, they, nonetheless, revealed the real motives of the Kuomintang's Marxist allies. The Comintern had issued secret instructions to the Chinese Communist Party, instructions which did not long remain secret: "Fight against the right wing of the Kuomintang; organize the left wing in common unity; and criticize the center." The Russians had also established the Sun Yat-sen University in Moscow to train their own cadre of Chinese agitators. Those "Russian returned students" were later to be a major source of friction within the Communist Party. At the time, the creation of the Sun Yat-sen University signaled to the Kuomintang that the Soviets were, to say the least, not wholly sincere in their promises of unselfish cooperation. Setting up a school for agitators hardly supported the Kremlin's stated aims. Moscow had declared its unqualified support of the "national revolution" and had repeatedly reaffirmed its belief that China was not yet ripe for Communism—and would not be ripe for decades.

The bluff and apparently candid Borodin had underscored the point when he refused an invitation to lecture to the students of the Canton Christian College on Communism, because he did not feel the subject was pertinent.

"Communism," the professional revolutionary told the American president of the Christian College, "is a philosophy and an ideal for which China is far from ready. China is a hundred years behind the times. From skyscrapers to rickshaws—what a contrast!"

The conservatives in the Kuomintang could not reconcile the Kremlin's disavowal of any desire to impose Communism on China with its secret instructions to the Chinese Communists and the founding of an academy for agitators in Moscow. Each side was suspicious of the other's intentions—and both sides were right.

Since the Chinese Communists were still in the leading strings of the Soviet Union and were themselves even more confused than their foreign masters as to the exact strategy of the revolution, the first open act which threatened the coalition came from the Kuomintang. The right wing of the Nationalist Party met in extended session in December, 1925, in the beautiful rolling Western Hills on the outskirts of Peking. Since the capital was not to fall to the Revolutionary Army for another thirty months, the warlord government was sympathetic to a gathering which might split their increasingly formidable enemies. The right wing fulfilled the expectations of its reluctant hosts. A formal resolution condemned the

Communists and demanded that Michael Borodin and General Galen be dismissed. The fight had come into the open.

Despite his sympathy with the right wing, the cautious Chiang was still not yet ready for an open break. An elaborate charade followed, as confusing to the uninitiated as a Peking Opera. In January, 1926, the Kuomintang's Second National Congress, including a large Communist representation, rejected the Western Hills proposal—and expelled leading members of the right wing from the Nationalist Party. But, in March, Chiang arrested the Communist captain and fifty crew members of the small warship *Chungshan*. He charged that they had mutinied.

Less than a month later, Chiang personally reaffirmed the solidarity of Chinese Communist Party–Kuomintang cooperation in a major public statement. Yet he had, in the interim, moved troops into Canton and executed a number of Communists and left-wing Nationalists. The moderates under Wang fled, for the conflict between Nationalists and Communists was also bringing to a head the personal conflict between Chiang Kai-shek and Wang Ching-wei. With the left wing out of the way, Chiang confirmed his alliance with the right wing, which he had, only months earlier, denounced. In May, 1926, the rump Central Executive Committee of the Kuomintang ejected Communists from all executive positions in the Nationalist Party and severely restricted their representation in the deliberative councils.

Although Secretary-General Ch'en pleaded with the Communist Party's Central Committee to repudiate the alliance with the Nationalists, the majority still gave unthinking loyalty to Moscow. Convinced, even against their own inclinations, that big brother knew best, the Comintern bloc within the Chinese Communist Party rejected their Secretary-General's proposal. Despite his bitterness, Ch'en, the schoolmaster and publicist turned politician, composed an open letter to Chiang, affirming Communist loyalty to the "national revolution" and denying any intention of sabotaging the joint cause. The Chinese Communist Party's Central Committee itself issued an even more effusive declaration of loyalty to the Kuomintang, calling on "revolutionary people of all classes to strengthen the people's united front."

Secretary-General Ch'en was himself later to plead that both the letter and the Central Committee's declaration had been extracted from the Chinese by Comintern pressure. At the time, it appeared to those who could follow the intricacies, to be an almost inexplicable act of near self-destruction. Even the Comintern itself was troubled, for a special meeting in November, 1926, sought to shape a new strategy for China—the chief proving ground of revolutionary tactics.

There were still some logical reasons for the apparently irrational behavior of both the Communists and the left wing of the Kuomintang. They did, after all, command a number of military units, while Whampoa graduates loyal to their cause occupied key positions in other divisions. Moreover, the left wing-Communist alliance unquestionably possessed a far greater measure of administrative talent than did the center and right wing group of the Kuomintang.

The leftist group also possessed the trappings of legality. After fleeing Canton in the spring of 1926, Wang, still officially chairman of the Nationalist Party, established his Provisional Government of China in Hankow, one of the triplet Wuhan cities, in November of 1926. He was supported not only by the presence of Michael Borodin, but also by such major figures as Soong Ching-ling, the widow of Sun Yat-sen, and his brilliant

Foreign Minister, Eugene Chen, an overseas Chinese from Jamaica. (Chen's lawyer son, Percy, was, many years later, to be the Communists' front man in British Hong Kong.) Moreover, Chinese trained in Moscow were returning to China to rally around the Hankow Government. The fight appeared, at the very least, to be met on equal terms.

In January, 1927, Liu Shao-c'hi, the future president of the Communist People's Republic, organized labor demonstrations in Hankow which ultimately led to Chinese occupation of the British Concession. The Hankow Labor Federation, Communist-controlled, was a major source of the strength of the Hankow government. Mao Tse-tung was active in Hunan to the south, organizing "farmers' associations" and preparing his influential *Report on The Peasant Movement* in a province fertile in both crops and revolutionists.

Despite his skill in maneuver, Chiang felt himself imperiled. He had taken Shanghai in March, 1927, in part by striking a secret deal with Chinese and foreign "capitalist elements." But the Communists had also played a major role in the conquest of the city which was, at once, the center of financial power and the symbol of China's humiliation under foreign domination. Secretary-General Ch'en Tu-hsiu and labor leader Liu Shao-ch'i had joined with Political Commissar Chou En-lai to organize the militant working class of the city into a People's Militia. The militia had disarmed the demoralized warlord troops and delivered an open city to the crack troops of Chiang's 118th Kwangsi Division. The classic Communist weapon of a proletarian uprising in a major city was, thus, for the first—and only—time successful in China.

During early April, 1927, the People's Militia still patrolled Shanghai, proud of their red arm bands and their rifles. The Kwangsi Division was camped outside the city, while Chiang conferred with the Communist leaders of the Shanghai commune—and, secretly, with capitalists and the powerful extra-legal "Red Band" secret society.

On April 12th, Chiang was ready to strike. Secret society gangsters joined the Kwangsi Division at four in the morning, and the combined force moved against the People's Militia. The countrymen from mountainous Kwangsi, disdainful of the slick Shanghailanders, gleefully obeyed Chiang's orders to disarm the workers without excessive gentleness. By noon, the "proletarian vanguard" was fleeing through the narrow streets and alleys, pursued by regulars firing rifles and submachine guns. The Nationalist forces finally converged on the headquarters of the Shanghai Federation of Labor Unions, where stubborn militia units held their last citadel under Chou En-lai until most were slaughtered.

Secretary-General Ch'en and labor leader Liu escaped before the final battle. Chou was captured—but was released by a former student, a Whampoa officer who was a secret Communist sympathizer. Chiang had, it appeared, broken decisively with the Communists and made his peace with "Chinese exploiters and foreign imperialists." But the break was still not total, largely because the Comintern refused to accept the obvious.

Still intoxicated by the illusion of installing a subservient Kuomintang government, the Comintern insisted that the Chinese Communist Party must continue to collaborate with the moderates of the Kuomintang. Although even the left wing of the Kuomintang was disillusioned with the Communists, Joseph Stalin, himself just winning the power struggle in Moscow, directed the Chinese Communists to maintain the alliance. The left-wing Hankow Government was itself suppressing Communist-inspired peasant risings with great bloodshed.

But Stalin insisted that the Chinese peasants be sacrificed on the altar of Chinese Communist Party–Kuomintang cooperation. His capacity for self-deception was demonstrated when he repeated his instructions to the Communists to collaborate with the Kuomintang—and then destroy it. Stalin's telegraphed instructions were mildly ambiguous. The Comintern representative who had replaced Michael Borodin, an Indian named M. N. Roy, therefore felt he could reassure the Hankow Government as to the Communists' loyalty by showing the telegram to Wang Ching-wei, chief of that government. Wang was, understandably, shocked—and the split between the Communists and the left-wing Kuomintang became inevitable.

Rarely had a campaign been so badly mismanaged. Instead of combining against their common enemy, the Nationalist right wing, the Communists and the moderates fought each other. It was a summer of fearful confusion. While Chiang marched, Moscow fumed and the Chinese Communist Party led peasant revolts and urban riots throughout Central China. Their fury was directed against Wang and the moderates, rather than against Chiang and the rightists. Emotion, rather than reason, governed their strategy. All Chiang's enemies were divided, not only from each other, but internally. All were in disarray: the Comintern, the Kuomintang's left wing, and the Communist Party of China. In July, 1927, Wang demanded the expulsion of the Communists from the Kuomintang. With his enemies totally disrupted, Chiang's victory was assured.

Sun Yat-sen's revolution was being completed under conditions that might have appalled him. The full irony was not yet displayed. Wang once more made cause with Chiang. But the Hankow liberals, led by Madame Sun Yat-sen, the youthful and attractive Soong Ching-ling,

and Foreign Minister Eugene Chen, fled to—of all places
—Moscow. Since many leading Communists also chose
exile, the field was clear for Chiang and his right-wing
allies.

But the Communists still had one shot in their locker
—armed revolt. On August 1st, 1927, Communist-led
troops rose in revolt in the capital of Kiangsi Province,
the old walled city of Nanchang. A new phase in the
Chinese revolution had begun, though the Nanchang
Revolt itself was to be a spectacular failure.

CHAPTER 4

To the Hills and the Alleys

MICHAEL BORODIN HAD returned to Moscow in a motorcade across the Gobi Desert. The Soviet capital, where Stalin was completing his own victory over Leon Trotsky, was host to scores of fugitive Chinese, both Communists and moderates. Borodin offered only one piece of bitter advice.

"The next time a Chinese general comes to Moscow talking of world revolution," he said, "the best thing to do is send for the Secret Police. The Chinese are only interested in guns."

Stalin had contrived the dreadful muddle himself by believing that he could manipulate both the Communists and the Nationalists for the greater glory of the Soviet Union. The illusion that the Chinese could be manipulated was later to generate equally disastrous errors by Soviet and Japanese governments, as well as the West, particularly the United States. But, even in late 1927, Stalin could not comprehend the immediate lesson, much less the long-range lesson, because he could not admit his mistakes—even to himself. The Kremlin's continuing inept meddling, so different from the world's image of the inhumanly efficient Marxist-Leninist conspiracy, was to spread confusion and dismay through the ranks of Chinese Communism for the next decade. The Communist Party of China, six years old in the summer of 1927, had not only split with the Nationalists and, to a degree, fallen out with the Comintern, but was bitterly divided against itself.

The last unified action of the Chinese Communist Party was, characteristically, a rather pointless armed revolt, which actually compelled the formal division of the Party into two mutually antagonistic wings.

On the morning of August 1st, 1927, the Communists had lost almost all formal power, but still retained a strong—if diffused—influence within the army through their cadre of indoctrinated officers. Just before dawn, the old walled city of Nanchang, lying in a narrow plain among the jagged mountains of Kiangsi Province, woke to the sound of gunfire. The cadets of the Nanchang Campus of the Whampoa Military Academy had risen in revolt against the Nationalists under the leadership of their commandant, Chu Teh. The commandant, whose name meant Red Virtue, was a veteran warlord general though he was just forty-four years old. He had been won away from a life of dissipation with opium and concubines by his conversion to Communism during an involuntary period of study in Germany. Although he adhered to the new doctrine with the total zeal of a convert, he retained the easy manners of his earlier profession and was beloved because of his concern for his troops. Personal loyalty, therefore, combined with political idealism and patriotic fervor to impel the young cadets to wholehearted participation in the revolt.

Seizing the city of Nanchang was easy. Brigades under
the secret Communist generals, Ho Lung and Yeh T'ing,
supported the cadets, while Chou En-lai reappeared
from the "underground" obscurity he had courted since
his escape from Shanghai, to lend his political counsel.
Among the Whampoa officers who cast their lot with the
rebels that day was a captain just twenty years old who
was an acting battalion commander. His name was Lin
Piao, and he had just joined the Communist Party, after
brief membership in the Socialist Youth Corps. A general before he was twenty-five, Lin Piao was to play a
major role in the subsequent military life of the Communist movement. He would initially emerge as the
Communists' most effective field commander and, later,
as the chief claimant to succession to the supreme power
of Mao himself.

Those events were, of course, hidden in the mists
of the future when the twenty thousand Communist
troops contemplated their successful revolt. The prospects were gloomy, though the victory had been swift.
They knew that they could not hold Nanchang against
the forces Chiang was already marshaling. Besides, retaining Nanchang under siege, if they could do so, would
in itself not materially contribute to the Communist
conquest of power over China. The gesture had been
splendid, and August First was, thereafter, to be cele-
brated as the anniversary of the founding of the Communist armed forces. But the immediate political and
military consequences were obscure, if not actually disastrous.

The Communists had thrown away one of their chief
advantages by unmasking their secret adherents within
the officer corps. The chief problem was no longer what
to do about Nanchang, but how to preserve the armed
nucleus which had made itself vulnerable by casting off

its camouflage. The great and glorious history of the Red Army of China, later called the People's Liberation Army, thus began with an apparent victory which led to a dead end. The same army was, ultimately, to win total victory after a series of apparent defeats. Political warfare, as so many conventional generals have learned to their discomfiture, is quite different from ordinary warfare.

The rebel forces finally decided to march southward toward Canton in the hope of finding allies and a base they could hold. While they were preparing for their departure, a splinter group of the Central Committee intensified the Communists' confusion and disunity by taking time out for a political housecleaning inspired partly by personal revenge.

Their victim was Secretary-General Ch'en Tu-hsiu, the man who had fought against blind obedience to the Comintern's orders to collaborate with the Nationalists. He was indicted for following the policies he had opposed, while a representative of the Comintern, which had originated those policies, joined his vengeful Chinese comrades in pronouncing judgment upon him. Ch'en, the moving spirit of the Communist Party from the beginning, was removed from his post, and a second-rank littérateur subservient to Moscow was installed in his place.

Ch'en had already resigned from his post in July, 1927, declaring: "The Comintern wishes us to carry out our own policy on the one hand and forbids us to leave the Kuomintang on the other. Under the circumstances, I see no way of carrying on and wish to be relieved of my duties." But The Emergency Meeting of August 7th, its legality highly questionable, insisted upon removing him formally.

Mao, who was one of the moving spirits in the attacks

on his old mentor, could take a certain satisfaction in Ch'en's humiliation and in winning perfunctory support for his own policy of basing the revolution upon the peasantry, rather than the urban proletariat or armed force. But he was disappointed in his own ambitions. The degradation of Ch'en, who had earlier disciplined him, placed the thirty-three-year-old Mao no closer to the center of power. He was, instead, ordered to Szechway Province in the far southwest to begin building up Communist strength among the farmers of China's largest and most fertile province.

Mao refused to obey. While the rebels of Nanchang began their withdrawal southward, Mao hastily assembled the activists he had recruited while serving as virtual chief of the Hunan Provincial Branch of the Chinese Communist Party during the preceding five years. Although he had, implicitly, opposed the policy of military insurrectionism exemplified by the Nanchang Rising, his own strategy now appears as hasty and ill-founded. Moved by the weakness for sudden, overwhelming enthusiasms he later displayed even more dramatically, Mao had convinced himself that the farmers of Hunan were ripe for revolt against their landlords and the government. He ordered all peasant organizations to rise in arms—though it was not clear what he hoped to accomplish. If trained Communist troops could not hold the fortress city of Nanchang, it was highly unlikely that peasant irregulars could hold the entire open Hunan plain—if, indeed, they could even gain control of the area.

The Harvest Rising of September, 1927, has become as sanctified in Communist mythology as the August First Rising at Nanchang, largely because it was organized by Mao himself. But the reality was quite different from the later idealized picture. The authorities crushed Mao's revolt with almost as little effort as a boy swatting a troublesome mosquito. The local warlord had become respectable by allying himself with the Nationalists, but found no need to call upon outside support. To his final humiliation, Mao was himself captured by a company of local militia. Not even regular troops, the militia should have been on his side. The only redeeming feature from Mao's standpoint was the slackness of the militia unit. Before they had identified him as the Communist chieftain of the province and the leader of the revolt, Mao managed to fall behind the main body by pretending that he had injured his leg. He bribed the militiaman who had been assigned to guard him and escaped into the hills.

Although Mao was, at least, free, he stood amid the debris of all his hopes. The Harvest Rising had failed, destroying Communist strength in Hunan. He was himself a lone fugitive who had alienated himself from the Central Committee of the Chinese Communist Party by disobeying its orders to go to Szechwan—and, even worse, by contriving defeat, rather than victory in Hunan. It was his blackest hour, though he still believed himself uniquely inspired to "liberate" China.

The remnants of the Nanchang rebels were still straggling southward, their numbers depleted by desertion, battle and illness, for they were constantly harassed by Nationalist troops. Some units under Ho Lung split off to find refuge in the hills of Kiangsi Province on the Hunan border. Others made for coastal Fukien. Still others, under Chu Teh and Yeh T'ing, doggedly worked their way toward southerly Kwangtung Province. They were soon reduced to a few thousand dispirited remnants. But the suicidal desire to stand and fight encouraged by the Comintern's conflicting orders had by no means burned itself out.

It almost seems when looking at the historical record that the Communists were determined to destroy themselves utterly in that hectic autumn and winter of 1927. But events, quite obviously, had a totally different appearance to the men who took part in them, for their vision was obscured by their own ambitions. Besides, they lacked the gift of hindsight which enables historians, comfortably ensconced in their library chairs, to discern the "inevitable" direction of events. The Communists, therefore, simply continued to fight. They were convinced that China was ripe for revolution—their revolution. They were, it was finally proved, wrong—just as wrong as it would be to assume that they should have known better because history is logical. Actually, the "logic of history" seemed to be in their favor at the time.

The peasants and workers of southern China, having been stirred to new hopes by the skillful propaganda of the Political Units of the Revolutionary Army, were moved by great discontent in the latter half of 1927. Their hopes were being dashed by the interplay of forces greater than themselves—the Communist International, the battered Chinese Communist Party, and the triumphant Kuomintang. But they could still be lured into following the Pied Pipers of revolution—because they wanted to be convinced.

The First Soviet Region, as the Communists called the areas where they established control, came into existence in November, 1927. Ho Lung's troops had occupied Swatow in northern Kwangtung Province in the middle of September, having come 350 miles from Nanchang. A Revolutionary Committee was established, and a Communist regime was proclaimed. It promptly declared war on the Nanking government. But Ho Lung was driven from Swatow in October by the combined pressure of foreign gunboats from the sea and Nationalist troops from the landward side. Nonetheless, he left his mark.

Under a dynamic leader called P'eng Pai, the Communists established an independent regime in the area just south of Swatow in northern Kwangtung Province between the towns of Haifeng and Lufeng. The names describe the area with bitter irony, for they mean Riches of the Sea and Riches of the Land. Actually, it was a poor and barren stretch of coast, depending for a living half upon the fish taken from the rough sea in clumsy, broad-prowed junks and half upon the meager yield of the infertile soil. If such conditions truly made the peasants ripe for revolt, they also insured that the Soviet Area could not endure. Lacking any real internal resources and beset by Nationalist forces, the Hailufeng First Soviet Area lasted only until February, 1928. Four months was the total life span of the first Communist government in China.

Four months was, however, a long span in comparison with the duration of the Canton Commune, the Communists' second experiment in urban government by a Revolutionary Committee. On December 1st, 1927, revolt broke out in the great port city which was the center of Communist strength among the workers, the old base of the Kuomintang, and, for centuries, China's chief point of contact with the outside world. P'eng Pai, fresh from his triumph, was a leader of the new revolt. Success had, it appeared, crowned his first attempt to establish a Communist-ruled region, and that success attracted other senior Communist leaders to Canton. The spark that united the revolt was the arrival of General Yeh T'ing, one of the three leaders of the Nanchang Rising. Still followed by a few thousand troops, General Yeh was

appointed commander-in-chief of the legions of the revolution. But the chief force was to be the militant workers,
and that force failed the Communists.

Since 1925 and the great demonstrations against the
British which had solidified the labor movement, the
Communist high command—and their Nationalist opponents—had reckoned Communist strength in Canton
at not less than 150,000 stalwart workers. But no more
than 10,000 responded when the Communists sounded
the trumpet of revolt and proclaimed their own government. Within three days, the Canton Commune was
crushed by regular Nationalist forces. The Nationalists
slaughtered most of the workers and utterly destroyed
the remaining troops of General Yeh T'ing, who fled
from China into exile which would end only after ten
years. The last Communist force in China appeared to
have been destroyed. Dr. Sun's dream of a united Nationalist-Communist alliance creating a new China was
totally dissipated in Canton, the city where the dream
had first appeared capable of becoming reality.

But a new force was already beginning to form in the
jagged and nearly impenetrable hills of Kiangsi Province, about 200 miles from Nanchang, where the abor-
tive revolt had occurred in August. One wing of the
rebel forces was still in existence, commanded by General
Chu Teh, the man whose name means Red Virtue. It
had been battered and harried until it mustered no
more than a thousand, including walking wounded. But
it was still a trained force under a commander who had
established a major reputation for tactical cunning and
human concern long before he revealed himself as a
Communist by joining the Nanchang Rising. After the
suppression of the Swatow Commune, Chu Teh and his
troops went to earth in Lochang County, on the border
of Hunan and Kwangtung Provinces. Since his troops

were as welcome as was his own presence, Chu Teh had no difficulty in making an alliance with a local military commander, who was still at least half a warlord, officially committed to the Nationalist government, but alert to his own advantage. Of all the defeated generals of Nanchang, only Chu Teh had found a firm territorial base.

Appointed a regimental commander and given command of the area, Chu began the time in his life which later Party historians were to describe as "ten years of preparation and cultivation." Almost instinctively, he initiated the strategy which was to win China. He began to extend his territorial base and to enlarge his army. During the winter of 1927-1928, when his fellow Communists were fleeing, Chu took control of several additional counties, some in Hunan to the north and others in Kiangsi to the northeast. He finally broke with the warlord who had given him refuge—so that he might pursue his own purpose. He was building a secure military base held by his own Workers' and Peasants' Red Army and developing the tactics which were later to win all China for the Communists.

The mountains were high and remote—hardly worthy of attention from the Nationalist commanders who had crushed the Swatow Commune, the Hailufeng Soviet Area, and the Canton Commune in their exposed positions. Chu Teh, however, depended as much upon the discontented peasantry of the barren area as he did upon concealment. Instead of building an army that lived upon the people, he knit civilians and soldiers into one force. The stocky, good-humored warlord turned Communist had learned the one lesson Chiang Kai-shek would never master. He knew that he was fighting a political war and that he was, therefore, dependent upon the good will of the peasants. He cultivated that good will with ostentatious benevolence—and imposed strict discipline upon his troops. For the first time in centuries, Chinese soldiers did not prey upon Chinese civilians.

But Chu Teh was operating in a virtual vacuum. The Central Committee of the Chinese Communist Party was hardly more aware of his existence or his potential than were the Nationalists. The seed of the revolution was sprouting unseen. One additional advantage was required before Chu Teh's sapling could begin growing toward maturity.

Mao Tse-tung, too, had become a fugitive after the failure of his Harvest Rising. But, unlike Chu Teh, he was quite alone until he finally encountered a band of fugitives on the border between Hunan and Kiangsi Provinces. Not even Communist-led, they were simple farmers joined together to follow the Red Flag raised by Mao Tse-tung. The group of a few hundred was broken, dispirited, fearful, and desperate. Still they all knew of Mao Tse-tung, and, remarkably, they did not blame him for their plight.

The tall, awkward rebel rose to stand among the lesser rebels sprawling on the hard ground. He was painfully thin, and his gestures were angular. His skin sagged on his big frame, and his long hair was greasy and lank.

"Comrades!" he exhorted, gesturing with his bony hands. "We have evaded the enemy. . . . How can he now harm us? After all, he is but mortal like us, and each enemy soldier has only two arms and two legs. When Comrade Ho Lung rose in revolt, he had two kitchen knives—and no troops. We have much more. We have nearly two battalions. How can you fear that we will not succeed?"

The tired rebels rose to the words Mao had learned to use so effectively during his days as an agitator. Since they would be killed if they were captured, they required of their leader only that he give them another chance for life—and, perhaps, victory.

Mao Tse-tung promised much to forge those broken remnants into the core of his own armed forces. Leading them by forced marches, he entered the Chingkangshan Mountain Range, which stretches some 200 miles within Kiangsi along the Hunan border. The area was accessible only through five narrow passes—and its natives were among the most backward farmers of China.

Mao Tse-tung maintained himself uneasily through the hard winter of 1927-1928, slightly extending the area under his control and beating off occasional Nationalist attacks. Like Chu Teh's, his area hardly seemed worth besieging. The Nationalists felt they had trapped Mao Tse-tung in a corner where they could leave him until they destroyed him at their leisure. But, in the spring of 1928, Chu Teh's better organized troops, a regiment strong, joined Mao's peasant irregulars in the Chingkangshan Range. The two forces became the nucleus of the Red Army.

Reorganized as the First Front Army of the Workers' and Peasants' Red Army, it was generally called the Chu-Mao Army by the local peasants. The two men were to work so closely together that it was several years before it became widely known that they were not a single individual. Mao Tse-tung had found his revolutionary base in the countryside, and the Communist movement in China had found the strategy which was, after two further decades, to carry it to victory.

CHAPTER 5

Warlords, Crushed
to Earth, Will . . .

ALTHOUGH THE COMMUNISTS officially reject the belief,
almost all Chinese are believers in what some scholars
call the "devil theory" and others call the "great man
theory" of history. That theory maintains that certain
great individuals, coming upon the stage of history at
crucial moments, totally alter the plot of the drama. The
Chinese are strongly inclined to that belief because their
own society changed only gradually and their formal history was dominated by the great figures of emperors,
ministers, rebels, and generals. They are, therefore, particularly sympathetic to the view that it is not some deep-
flowing stream of inevitability which shapes the destiny
of men and nations, as Marxism asserts, but rather the
deeds of great individuals, acting for good or for evil.
The Chinese were, significantly, the first people to make
detailed biographies a major section of their official
chronicles. While formally rejecting the "great man"
theory of history in obedience to Marxist doctrine, even

the Communists have shown the same strong inclination toward the belief that certain supreme figures determine men's fate—as demonstrated, to give one example, by their near deification of Mao Tse-tung.

Two great men certainly dominated the tumultuous years from the death of Dr. Sun Yat-sen in 1925 to the establishment of the People's Republic of China in 1949. They were, of course, Mao Tse-tung himself, and his great rival, Chiang Kai-shek.

The Communist leader was the son of a rich farmer, a class he was later to attack, while the Nationalist leader was the son of the prosperous minor gentry. Chiang's family did not quite belong to the upper classes, for there were few senior officials or wealthy merchants listed on its sacred ancestral tablets. But it was far above Mao's family in the Chinese social system, since it included distinguished scholars and middle-rank officials in its chronicles. Chiang Kai-shek also received the formal education Mao never quite attained, having been an honor student at the Japanese Military Academy.

As stubborn and self-righteous as Mao Tse-tung, Chiang Kai-shek displayed one quality which his agile rival lacked. His critics call it inflexibility, while his champions call it loyalty. Regardless of how commentators characterize that trait in his personality, Chiang remained true in his allegiance to his beliefs and his superiors. Despite an agility in intrigue which equaled Mao Tse-tung's, Chiang Kai-shek staunchly supported Sun Yat-sen from the Revolution of 1911 until his mentor's death. In this constancy, he was quite unlike Mao, who never acknowledged a superior and, indeed, gleefully participated in the degradation of Secretary-General Ch'en Tu-hsiu. Chiang's later adherence to the Three Principles of the People is, of course, questionable. His presumed intention to carry out Dr. Sun's plan was, perhaps, as distorted by the weight of circumstances as was Mao's belief in the principles of Marxism.

Chiang's course was, moreover, by no means straight, for he was proceeding amid the intricate complexities of Chinese intrigue. The summer of 1927, which had seen his own military victories and the dispersion of the Communists, found Chiang himself in political difficulties. He was forced by the pressure of his enemies within the Kuomintang to surrender supreme command to a triumvirate of rival generals. Much jealousy undoubtedly had been aroused by the abrupt rise to power of the 42-year-old Generalissimo, who was still hardly more than a stripling by Chinese standards. Besides opposition from the diehards of the extreme right, Chiang came under the suspicion of the moderates and the surviving "left-wing" members of his party. They feared that he might seek to replace the warlords he was supplanting, making himself a super-warlord ruling all China, who could disregard the will of the Kuomintang as he wished.

Chiang accepted this reverse with the same calm self-confidence he was to display in similar circumstances later in his career. First, his belief in his own destiny told him that he would soon regain his position. The nation, as well as the Kuomintang, needed him badly, since the Northern Expedition was still not concluded. In the second place, the history of China abounded in examples of successful statesmen retiring gracefully to cultivate their own gardens when confronted by the malice of their enemies. Many of those statesmen had later returned to triumph. Finally, the young Chiang Kai-shek had important personal business to transact. His enforced respite from the responsibilities of power, therefore, did not dismay him unduly.

Although he had been married twice, once to a "village bride" selected by his parents, and was the father of two sons, Chiang's inclinations had turned to the beautiful, American-educated daughter of one of the wealthiest men in China. She was named Soong Mei-ling. Her father, called Charlie Soong, was a banker with a multitude of foreign connections, having been one of the first Chinese to study in the United States. Her elder sister, Soong Ching-ling, was the widow of Dr. Sun Yat-sen and a member of the extreme left wing of the Kuomintang. Soong Mei-ling herself was a vivacious and highly intelligent girl of 26, with a desire for power almost as strong as Chiang's own. She was also a devout Methodist, a trait mildly disturbing to the traditionalistic Confucianist Chiang Kai-shek.

His personal problems were resolved when he journeyed to Japan in October, 1927, to formally ask Mei-ling's hand of her mother, who was convalescing from a serious illness in the Island Kingdom. Having already won the affection of the daughter herself, he found Madame Soong quite happy to consent to Mei-ling's marriage to the man who already appeared the most likely successor to her deceased son-in-law, Sun Yat-sen. Chiang, for his part, was converted by his fiancée to Methodism, a creed from which he never wavered through the difficult years that followed. Though he remained Confucian in his devotion to the age-old virtues of Chinese society and in his strict standards of personal behavior, Chiang Kai-shek could become a devout Methodist. There was no basic contradiction, since Confucianism was not really a religion, but a personal and political philosophy.

Chiang's journey to Japan, characteristically, had a two-fold purpose. The Japanese had been playing an ever more intrusive role in China since the beginning of the first World War in 1914. They had extended their influence from their colony of Korea into China's northeastern provinces of Manchuria, playing the game of making and breaking warlords with even greater relish than did their Western co-imperialists. It was, Chiang felt, essential to obtain Japanese toleration—if not outright support—of his plans to unify China by taking Peking. After speaking with the Japanese Prime Minister, he came away with an agreement which was never made public. In broad outline, the agreement appears to have granted the Japanese a reasonably free hand in Manchuria in return for their tacit support in China proper—and their promise to leave the territory south of the Great Wall to the Nationalists.

Although his faith in the Japanese agreement was, in the long run, to prove unfounded, Chiang's confidence in his own indispensability was well founded indeed. Shortly after his return to China with his new bride, he once again took command of the Revolutionary Army—and the Revolutionary Army soon took Peking.

But all his contrived alliances were creaking. Having broken with his Communist allies, he found that his warlord allies were breaking with him. After Chiang had taken Peking in June, 1928, with their assistance, the Christian General Feng Yü-hsiang and the "Model Governor" of Shansi Province, Yen Hsi-shan, realized that he was not merely another warlord seeking personal power. Chiang Kai-shek showed himself a major threat to the established warlords. He had truly undertaken the mission left by Sun Yat-sen—to unite the nation and rule over it. He was determined to use his power to produce a centrally ruled China governed according to the Three People's Principles. Chiang's single-mindedness upset the balance of power throughout the country. The remaining warlords, having pledged their loyalty to the Nationalist cause, reckoned correctly that Nationalist

policies were planned to destroy their special privileges
—and, ultimately, their positions.

Growing tension between the local warlords and the
central government in Nanking became acute at the
Demobilization Conference of January, 1929. The
Northern Expedition having ended with the conquest of
power, Chiang was prepared to reduce his forces, for he
considered the Communists only a minor threat. He indicated that he expected the warlords to follow his example, though he knew that their position was quite different from his own. As the chief of the single legitimate
government, which would still maintain a formidable
army, Chiang could expect to retain his power after demobilization. Indeed, his power would increase. The
warlords' own authority rested almost entirely on their
armed forces. If they demobilized their armies, they
would have no choice but to accept Chiang's overriding
authority. They would, in effect, become governors appointed by Nanking. Assuming power to appoint governors would implicitly give Nanking the right to discharge
governors.

The major warlords were not prepared to make such
submission to Chiang Kai-shek, despite their oaths of
loyalty to the Kuomintang and the Three People's Principles. The first major opposition, however, came not
from Generals Feng Yü-hsiang and Yen Hsi-shan in the
north, but from the generals of the so-called Kwangsi
Province Clique, whose troops had crushed the Shanghai
People's Militia for Chiang Kai-shek. Two of the chief
leaders of the Kwangsi Clique were arrested in Nanking
during the Demobilization Conference, one barely es-
caping by a Japanese freighter to British Hong Kong.
War between the center and the Kwangsi warlords became inevitable. It was the first of the battles Chiang was

to fight to establish his supreme authority and to subordinate the independent provinces to the central government in Nanking.

Chiang won his first battle against the regional forces
in quick time. By May, 1929, the Kwangsi Army was
defeated. His strategy, once again, was indirect. Though
the warlords of neighboring Kwangtung normally would
have supported the warlords in their sister province,
Chiang had won their support by promising to grant
them greater independence. Equally important, he had
neutralized the major threat of the Christian General
Feng Yü-hsiang in the north by promising him a free
hand in Shantung Province.

But the peace brought by the defeat of the Kwangsi
Clique endured only briefly. The suspicious Feng Yü-
hsiang declared himself commander-in-chief of the
"Northwest Army for Protection of the Kuomintang and
National Salvation" in late May, 1929. Chiang, once
again, staved off a major conflict by buying off Feng Yü-
hsiang's key supporters. But the lull was brief. By September, 1929, the southern warlords of Kwangtung and
Kwangsi began moving to consolidate their independent
positions against Chiang's obvious determination to
bring them under central control. One chief challenger
was defeated in Wuhan, while another remained quies-
cent for a time. It appeared that Chiang Kai-shek was
succeeding in his crafty policy of splitting his enemies—
taking two steps forward for every step backward.

The situation was, however, still too unstable to yield
either to his political adroitness or to his military tactics
of concentrating his troops to deal with one enemy at a
time. At the beginning of 1930, the Christian General
Feng Yü-hsiang and the Model Governor Yen Hsi-shan
united against Nanking in the north. In the south, General Li Tsung-jen of Kwangsi, later briefly vice-president

and acting president of the Republic of China, allied himself with General Chang Fa-k'uei, who had commanded the "Ironsides" Fourth Division during the Northern Expedition. The war on two fronts continued through September, 1930, involving more than a million troops, while draining both the funds and the energies of the Central Government. Chiang's predicament appeared desperate.

His worries were doubled by the sudden return of Wang Ching-wei, Sun Yat-sen's "legal" heir, to dispute the supreme authority Chiang had taken for himself. Wang Ching-wei brought together all his supporters within the Kuomintang to proclaim a separate "legal" National Government in Peking with himself at its head. But Chiang Kai-shek still had an ace in the hole. The Young Marshal of Manchuria, Chang Hsüeh-liang, marched his armies to Peking and crushed the new National Government. Chiang had, once again, come through apparently unscathed.

Nanking made an uneasy peace with the rebellious warlords by granting them broad autonomy, as well as offices in the central government. The maneuvering had set the pattern of Chiang Kai-shek's attempts to impose his own authority—and a central government upon China—for some years to come. Too weak militarily to crush the opposition, he was also too rigid and unimaginative politically to appeal directly to the people to create a firm base of government. Instead, he sought by constant political maneuvering to maintain his own position. It was, essentially, a policy of divide and rule, but it could not work effectively because Chiang was forced to concede too much power to his opponents. The natural regionalization of the vast country was, therefore, intensified. Chiang Kai-shek was never in reality the *Tsung-ts'ai* or Supreme Ruler, but only the first man among equals.

Only his acrobatic adroitness in intrigue made it possible for him to remain at the top of the pyramid of power.

Chiang's attempts to create a firm base for his government might, as has been suggested, have been more successful if he had been able to win popular support by carrying out the reforms Sun Yat-sen had promised. But he was hampered as much by his inflexible mentality as he was by his own precarious position. A Christian spiritually, he was a Confucian politically. Confucianism demanded that the common people give willing obedience to a strong central ruler. That ruler was, in turn, expected to act generously and confer many benefits on the people. But he was not supposed to take them into his confidence or inquire after their wishes. The doctrines of Sun Yat-sen actually reinforced Chiang's natural tendency toward autocracy, for the Three People's Principles had prescribed a "period of tutelage" before the general public could be considered fit to rule itself democratically. The authoritarian tendencies of the Kuomintang were thus legitimately derived from the man who was their political teacher.

Even if Chiang Kai-shek had truly wished to hasten democratic reforms, he probably could not have done so. His troubles were not limited to the restive warlords. By late 1930, Japanese pressure was becoming heavy on the northern tier of China. The Japanese had, it was obvious, made their original deal with Chiang in the expectation that he would later prove an easy nut for them to crack. Moreover, the Communists were becoming a major nuisance in Central China despite their own internal divisions. Chiang Kai-shek decided to deal with the lesser problem first. He felt that he must unite China under his own control, before he could cope with the Japanese. In November, 1930, he ordered the first of his Extermination Campaigns against the Soviet Areas of

Central China. The struggle between the Nationalists and the Communists was, once again, met on the battlefield.

Despite their internal splits and the interference of the Communist International, the Communists had made themselves a serious threat just three years after the debacle of the Nanchang Rising of August 1st, 1927. They enjoyed one great advantage which even their own clumsiness could not destroy. Chinese workers and farmers were even more discontented with their lot than they had been before the Northern Expedition marched. Fired by Communist propaganda, they would no longer accept the deprivation and suffering they had endured for a century and a half. Widespread resentment was the Communists' most powerful weapon.

CHAPTER 6

The Men
of the Mountains

MAO TSE-TUNG HAD never risen to the highest ranks of the Communist Party of China, although he was one of the twelve men who attended its first—and founding—National Congress in July, 1921.

The intellectuals had looked down upon his imperfect education, and he had worried the *apparatchiks*, the organization men, by his stubborn independence. You could, to paraphrase an American wisecrack, always tell Mao Tse-tung by his shock of bristling black hair and his spirited championing of his own views, but you could not tell him much. He was convinced that he was right when others disagreed with him, particularly when the entire Party apparatus disagreed. That characteristic, to say the least, made him difficult to work with and, even more serious, made him a misfit in a political party which enforced strict discipline on its members—whatever their rank. When the Party Center had spoken, all Communists were required to obey. But Mao Tse-tung, as often as not, defied the orders of the Party Center. He was several times punished by suspension from the Party, but he would not change.

In the spring of 1928, Mao Tse-tung was finally coming into his own. His course, thereafter, was to run ever forward towards great power within the CCP and the ultimate overlordship of all China. There were, however, to be many "twistings and turnings," as the Communists say, in Mao's progress to power. Despite the assertions of the later, "sanitized" accounts of his career produced by Communist publicists, he was by no means the automatic rallying point for all Communist loyalties after his forces joined those of General Chu Teh in the Chingkangshan Range in the spring of 1928. A hard struggle lay ahead—not merely the struggle to place Communism over China, but the struggle to place Mao over Communism in China.

Both Mao Tse-tung's inclinations and his training admirably qualified him for those struggles. He had, throughout his thirty-four years, always been at odds with authority, beginning with his early rebellions against his harsh and avaricious father. Although he had evaded his father's insistence that he join the family businesses of pig-raising and money-lending and had entered a "modern" primary school at the age of sixteen, his stay at that school had been brief. He had quarrelled bitterly with his history teacher, who doubted the historical truth of the youth's favorite reading—old, popular novels which told of the heroic struggles of rebels against authority. When his teacher explained that the novels were based on history, but were not themselves history, Mao was infuriated. His deepest beliefs had been threatened. He created such a furor that he was expelled. He would behave in exactly the same way in later crises in his life.

For a number of years, he drifted from school to school and from interest to interest, much like the hero of one of his cherished novels. He enlisted in the army about the time of the Revolution of 1911, but did not find service in the ranks pleasant. Finally, he was introduced to Communism, a doctrine which promised to make China great again—and also offered great opportunities to an ambitious and idealistic young man. He was working as a clerk in the library of Peking University when he was first exposed to Marxist doctrines, for the University was the center of advanced thought for all China. Again like a hero in the traditional novels he loved, he had found his cause.

The following years were full of adventure—and frustration. Mao found himself in opposition not only to the Kuomintang, but to his own Communist Party. Because of his nature, he enjoyed the fights. But they interfered with his advancement. It was not until he came to Chingkangshan in late 1927 that he was, finally, on his own. The reinforcements provided by the troops of General Chu Teh completed Mao's change from rebel to leader. Chu Teh was a soldier, not a politician, and he was happy to follow Mao's political dreams. For the first time, Mao Tse-tung at thirty-four could act as he wished. For the first time, he commanded his own troops and his own territory. He was even blessed, though distantly, by the Communist International's grudging approval of his personal strategy of basing the Chinese revolution on the peasantry and, subsequently, using the Red countryside to encircle and conquer the White cities.

Chingkangshan was safe because it was remote. But the area would hardly have appealed to a strategist as the best place to build an army that would eventually conquer China. Though it was an area rich in natural resources, no more than 2,000 country folk lived a primitive life in its five large villages. They grew rice, cotton, beans, and peanuts in the fertile soil, which was well watered by frequent rains. But the fir and bamboo forests were the kingdom of wild animals—not only deer, pheasant, beaver, and other edible game, but predatory beasts—tigers, leopards, wolves, and jackals. Still, Chingkangshan was Mao Tse-tung's kingdom too.

In the great world outside the remote retreat Mao Tse-tung and Chu Teh had chosen for themselves, great events were in progress. Most of those developments were disastrous for a Communist Party still reeling from its defeats.

Nonetheless, a new force was coming into being. In Pingchiang in Hunan Province, another Communist general who was to play a major role in Mao's life was making his own bid for independent power. In July, 1928, P'eng Teh-huai broke away from his Nationalist allegiance and raised the Red flag. The Pingchiang Soviet was thus established as the second Communist-ruled area in China. Other Communist generals created their own enclaves, notably Ho Lung, one of the leaders of the Nanchang Rising. Hsü Hsiang-ch'ien, also, whose political mentor was Chang Kuo-t'ao, another founding member of the CCP, was to contend with Mao for supreme power in the mid-1930s.

While the guerrilla forces, divided by geography and leadership, were growing almost spontaneously, the formal center of the Communist Party of China was reorganizing itself under Russian tutelage. In July, 1928, the Sixth National Congress of the CCP met. The setting was Moscow, partly because so many leading Communists had fled to asylum in the Soviet capital, and partly because there was no place in China where the Congress could deliberate undisturbed. Even the International Settlement of Shanghai, a refuge for rebels for genera-

tions, had closed its gates to the Communists. Chiang
Kai-shek had done a masterful job of isolating his enemies.

Yet the Sixth Congress was followed by a secret session
of the "legal" Central Committee and Political Bureau
of the CCP in Shanghai itself. Three men had emerged
from the Moscow meeting as the leading spirits of the
Party. Under a weak Secretary-General, they were: Chou
En-lai, chief of the Organization Department, later
premier; Liu Shao-ch'i, chief of the Labor Department,
later chairman (president) of the People's Republic;
and the spitfire Li Li-san, chief of the Propaganda Department. Although Li dominated the Political Bureau,
he had aroused too much antipathy to become Secretary-
General himself. Nonetheless, his tactics, later excoriated
by Mao's supporters as the "Li Li-san Line," were in the
ascendant—largely because the Sixth Congress, bullied
and confused by the Russians, had formulated no clear
strategy to meet the confused and difficult conditions the
CCP confronted.

The chief directive of the Sixth Congress included all
points of view, without really supporting any. Acknowl-
edging that a "rising revolutionary situation" did not yet
exist in China, the resolution nevertheless directed the
Party to stir up unrest among both the industrial and
agricultural proletariat. The Communists were commanded to lead widespread armed rebellions, though
they had just signally failed to win by that strategy and
lacked both weapons and popular support. The chief resolution of the Sixth Congress insisted that the main force
of the revolution must be the "urban proletariat," the
working people of the cities, although revolts in the cities
had already ended in disaster. The same resolution also
endorsed the "peasant movement." The Communists
were told not to make enemies of the rich peasants, but

still to build up "rural Soviet Areas." The conclusions of the Sixth Congress took account of everyone's views, including those of Mao Tse-tung's isolated "rural faction," but did not choose among them. By its very vagueness, it worked against any decisive action.

Neither the Sixth Congress nor the isolated Maoist faction had, however, reckoned with the impetuous Li Li-san. He scoffed at the cautious tactics of the "rural faction" and demanded immediate attacks against the cities of China, because they were the "centers of bourgeois strength." Li Li-san in 1929 displayed a power of imagination almost as great as that shown by Mao Tse-tung's later grandiose plans for "liberating all mankind" from the "firm base" of the weak, hedged-in People's Republic in the 1960s. Li argued that "capitalist imperialism" was on its last legs because of the worldwide economic depression. China, Li Li-san contended, was particularly ripe for revolt because her capitalists were completely dependent upon foreign support—economic, political and military. Once China fell to the crushing blows of the Communists, he concluded, imperialism would collapse of its own weight, for the exploitation of China was the prop which sustained "capitalist imperialism" throughout the world.

Commanding the "legal" Party apparatus in Shanghai, Li soon showed that he was not content merely to spin theories. He ordered the scattered Communist armies to attack the cities. The first such assault was staged against the old city of Changsha, the capital of Hunan, home province of both Li Li-san and Mao Tse-tung. The commander of the attack against Changsha in July, 1930, was General P'eng Teh-huai. His troops were called the Third Red Army Group, an imposing title for a force that numbered hardly more than ten thousand.

The Third Army Group was badly equipped, lacking

even the simplest radios. But P'eng had trained hard for the battle. The Communist leaders really believed that taking Changsha would be the first in a series of blows that would bring down the warlords and the Kuomintang; destroy the old order in China; and "liberate" the common people. They half believed that Changsha's fall would set off a shockwave that would bring down the old "capitalist-imperialist" order throughout the world. The enemy troops were neither moved by such grand visions nor inspired to the desperate courage of men who know that they will die if they do not win. Nonetheless, it was a hard fight before the Third Red Army Group finally broke the enemy's resistance and occupied Changsha.

The "Provisional Soviet Government for Hunan Province" was established with Li as its chairman. Decrees and laws came pouring out of the city for ten days as if it were actually the capital of a Communist-ruled province, rather than a besieged fortress in the midst of hostile territory. When the warlord and Kuomintang forces rallied, the Third Red Army Group was forced to retreat from Changsha. The first provincial Communist government, which never really ruled more than the city of Changsha, collapsed in less than two weeks. None of the glowing visions of Li Li-san had been realized.

But Li Li-san was a stubborn man. Like Mao Tse-tung, he was never convinced by defeat that he would not win in the end. Li argued that the "successful attack" against Changsha, the center of communications and commerce for south-central China, proved that continuing attacks on the cities would bring the capitalists crashing down. Under his influence, the Political Bureau passed a resolution noting "the new revolutionary high tide" and ordering a "multiprovincial offensive."

The CCP was thus committed to the "Li Li-san Line," a strategy of widespread "insurrectionism" to snatch quick victory from a feeble enemy. (Li Li-san's was much like the strategy behind the Tet Offensive of 1968 in South Vietnam. But his plans were neither as efficient as the Viet Cong's, nor were his opponents as shaken by his passing successes.) Although an attack against Nanchang on August 1st, 1930, was a complete failure, Li's strategy was still dominant. But, in September, the Li Li-san strategy broke against the same rock on which it had been founded. A second attack against Changsha was stopped while the Communist forces still stood outside the city walls. The Comintern had hailed the first battle for Changsha as "the commencement of a new chapter of the Chinese revolution," but second thoughts began to rise. Opposition within the CCP itself was becoming overwhelming.

Mao Tse-tung had been winning over the officers of Red Army units other than his own, beginning at a conference at Kutien in Fukien Province in late 1929. At Kutien he had used a combination of force and persuasion to establish his control of the military machine. He realized that he must destroy Li Li-san before he could take command himself. At Kutien, Mao denounced the "adventuristic" policy of attacking the cities, when the Red Army was still inadequately equipped and slackly disciplined. He declared that the Communists could only win by following his own policy of building up strong— if remote—rural bases in which to train the Red Army before they could even dream of attacking the cities.

Given much personal authority by his control of the single largest Soviet Area, Mao Tse-tung appeared with Chu Teh beneath the walls of Changsha during the second siege. Because the Communists had taken severe losses from the artillery, airplanes, and gunboats of the Nationalists, Mao persuaded the Red commanders to abandon the siege. Taken without permission from the

Party Center, the battlefield decision forced Li Li-san to abandon his "insurrectionist line."

A third group within the Party had already begun to protest against the reckless policy of Li Li-san, which imperiled the Red Army, the only real source of Communist strength. They were called the "Russian faction" because their nucleus was some two dozen young Chinese who had just returned from Moscow. Their leader was Wang Ming, who was later to be denounced by the Maoists for both "right-wing conservatism," and "left-wing adventurism." Their chief adviser and link to the Communist International was Pavel Mif. Itself still confused and disoriented, the "Russian faction" introduced a third element into the unstable balance of power within the Communist Party. It was opposed to both Mao Tse-tung's "rural faction" and Li Li-san's legal "Shanghai Center" in the developing power struggle. A fourth "Trotskyite faction" had formed around former Secretary-General Ch'en Tu-hsiu, but he was soon read out of the Party.

Unable to unite among themselves, the Chinese Communists could hardly expect to defeat their enemies. The Nationalists enjoyed the financial and diplomatic support of the foreign powers, as well as the intermittent loyalty of local leaders who were hardly more than legalized warlords. The fight appeared wholly unequal, a powerful, semi-centralized KMT against a splintered and scattered CCP.

Besides, the struggle within the Communist Party was just beginning. The man who was later to be premier of the People's Republic, Chou En-lai, was still loyal to Li Li-san. He scurried off to Moscow, the court of last resort, to defend his leader's position. But he arrived in Moscow *after* a telegram from Shanghai, signed by Pavel Mif, denouncing Li Li-san's policies for destroying the remaining strength of the CCP. Though the Comintern had not yet made up its mind, Chou En-lai hurried back to China to defend the "Shanghai Center" at a conference of the Central Committee held at Lushan in Kiangsi Province, a famous summer resort, in September, 1930. The issue was deferred until November 12th, 1930, when the "Russian faction" presented a new resolution, totally condemning Li Li-san. On November 16th, the long awaited message from the Comintern arrived. Moscow, too, condemned Li Li-san.

Their distant masters having spoken, the Chinese Communists came to heel on November 25th, 1930. The Comintern had condemned Li Li-san for his "adventuristic insurrectionism," but had not offered an alternative policy. The Chinese were, however, glad to receive guidance, however unclear. The internal struggle among equally balanced factions might otherwise have continued interminably. The Central Committee reprimanded Li for "unprincipled opportunism," which meant in plain language that he had failed. In January, 1931, he was removed from office and ordered to Moscow for "consultation"—not to return for almost 15 years.

Wang Ming, the leader of the "Russian faction," became Secretary-General, while the indestructible Chou En-lai, hastily repudiating his disgraced leader, became chief of the Military Affairs Bureau of the Central Committee. The shape of the future was dimly apparent after the series of conferences, whose decisions were all negative. The Party Center vaguely endorsed the policy of building up rural Soviet Areas. It called for a Congress of Soviet Representatives to meet in Juichin, the capital of the Kiangsi Soviet Area that Mao Tse-tung and Chu Teh had established after losing their original base in the Chingkangshan Range.

Mao Tse-tung was ready to move into the power vacuum, for he alone offered a positive policy. The "opportunistic adventurism" of Li had brought the Party's military offensive to a dead end. On the political front, the Party received no effective leadership from a Political Bureau that could not make up its own mind without consulting the Comintern. That body, far away in Moscow, was washing its hands of the messy "China Problem." Moscow was, in any event, fully occupied with its own problems after the battle for power between Leon Trotsky and Joseph Stalin. It seemed that Communists simply could not agree among themselves, even where they held "state power," as they did in the Soviet Union. But, at least, Mao Tse-tung, like Joseph Stalin, knew his own mind and his own desires. Like Stalin, Mao also knew exactly how to gather power into his own hands. Whatever its failings as a base for conquering China, the Kiangsi First Soviet Area gave Mao a firm base for conquering power within the Communist Party. By mid-1931 he had already brought most of the remnants of the Red Army under his predominant influence, though not yet under his direct command.

In late 1931, the delegates began to arrive in Juichin for the First Congress of Soviet Representatives. They came stealthily to the little mountain town which had become the capital of Communist China. They came from the scattered smaller Soviet Areas and from the "Party Center" in Shanghai. Among the delegates making their way by devious routes and in curious disguises to evade the Kuomintang's "special service" police were Chou En-lai and the Chinese Communist Party's new Secretary-General Wang Ming. But it was Mao Tse-tung's conference, for it was held on his home ground. The Communist Party was not itself meeting, but, rather, the representatives of the Soviet Areas. Mao Tse-tung's was, by far, the largest and most secure of those areas.

Mao Tse-tung's supreme power over his own Kiangsi Soviet Area was affirmed by the Congress through his election as chairman of the Soviet Government, while his right-hand man, General Chu Teh, was chosen chairman of the Soviet's People's Military Affairs Commission. Although there *were* other Soviet Areas, Mao was thus recognized as first, by far, among the equal leaders of all the Soviet Areas. He was not to attain formal leadership over the Party apparatus for some years to come, though Wang Ming soon returned to Moscow for "liaison duties," a strange assignment for the Secretary-General of the Communist Party of China.

The reality of power, that is, the supremacy of Mao Tse-tung, was demonstrated by two highly significant events. Chou En-lai, that seasoned intriguer, who had survived by his ability to sense the direction in which the political wind would blow *next*, left Shanghai to offer his services to Mao Tse-tung's Kiangsi Soviet. He soon became vice-chairman of the Soviet Military Affairs Commission.

At the same time, Chiang Kai-shek, another sensitive politician, was deeply disturbed by the series of attacks on cities, though they cast the Communist Party into confusion and almost destroyed its armed forces. Chiang decided to intensify his own military pressure on the Communists. He directed his most persistent attacks at the Kiangsi Soviet because it was both the strongest and the most dangerous.

CHAPTER 7

The Two Sieges

IN 1931, CHINA presented a picture of disunity that was truly spectacular. The Chinese, who never did things by halves, had outdone themselves. Their internal feuding was on such a grand and complex scale that it was almost something to boast about. If the largest country in the world were to fall into administrative and political chaos it was, perhaps, fitting that the scope of the confusion should be vast and intricate.

The Communists, as has been seen, were divided by policy differences and geographical distances. The Comintern still supported the shadowy, half-fugitive Central Committee in Shanghai, while a number of leaders in the countryside each claimed supreme power in their own independent Soviet Areas. Mao Tse-tung had, of course, made himself first among the "independent princes" of the Soviet Areas. But he could not command his fellow princes' total obedience.

Chiang Kai-shek found himself in a similar position

among the Nationalists. He was pressed not only by his opponents within the Kuomintang, but by independent warlords, who obeyed his orders only when it suited them. In 1931-32, Chiang was so hard-pressed by resistance and rebellion among the non-Communists that he ceremonially resigned his position as chief of state, while retaining military power. Under such conditions it was patently impossible for the Kuomintang to put into effect the reformed system of government envisioned by Dr. Sun Yat-sen.

Whether the Kuomintang truly had the desire to do so is, of course, another question. It can never be answered clearly because it is, quite simply, impossible to tell exactly *who* was the Kuomintang during that confused period. Certainly, the Nanking government would have liked nothing better than to extend its authority over the entire country and to push the economic construction which would make China strong. But Nanking could not do so. Internal and external pressures were too great.

The Japanese picked the moment of greatest confusion to begin clawing again at the northern flank of China. They had been quiet for a few years, perhaps because they felt that their presumed secret agreement with Chiang would give them what they wanted without fighting—until later. Like Chiang Kai-shek, the Japanese preferred to attain their aims by negotiation and intrigue. But, like Chiang Kai-shek, they would fight when they felt fighting was the only way to get what they wanted. In 1931, the ambitious Japanese military, already plotting to control all Asia, decided to strike decisively. Domination of Manchuria, followed by gradual penetration south of the Great Wall, would, in time, give them effective control over China, the heartland of Asia.

In September, 1931, the Japanese decided that talking had taken them as far as it could. They began an unde-

clared war against China which would continue until
1937, when it became a formal war.

The immediate cause of the first armed clashes was
growing Chinese strength in Manchuria, the three
northeastern provinces beyond the Great Wall. (The
broad plains of the northeast had been the home grounds
of the Manchu tribes which conquered China proper in
1644.) Increasing Chinese influence was bound to clash
with Japanese ambitions. Since the late 19th Century, an
overpopulated and overenergetic Japan had been pouring capital and settlers into Manchuria, developing both
an industrial complex and a spill-over basin for excess
population. Never an integral part of China, the area was
also an invaluable source of raw materials and a major
strategic base in the event of war with the Soviet Union,
Japan's traditional rival in Northeast Asia.

But the Chinese settlers had also been pouring into
the region—not just for decades, but for centuries. The
Manchurian government of the Young Marshal Chang
Hsüeh-liang was proving less cooperative than the Japanese had hoped. Chang had no reason to love them. The
Young Marshal had, after all, succeeded his father, Marshal Chang Tso-lin, after the latter was assassinated by
the Japanese Military Intelligence Service. Besides,
Chang Hsüeh-liang was too close to the Nanking government for Japanese tastes. He considered himself a
Chinese, rather than just a Manchurian.

The ambitious Japanese generals, therefore, required
only a suitable excuse to begin securing the riches of
Manchuria by armed force. They were actively seeking a
plausible reason for a sudden military strike such as they
had directed against Russian-held Port Arthur in 1904
and would direct against Pearl Harbor in 1941. Given
the desire, the pretext was not hard to find—or manufac-
ture.

Hundreds of thousands of Koreans, all Japanese citizens because their homeland was a Japanese colony, had sought more spacious farming lands in Manchuria. Their aggressive temperaments had brought them into conflict with the Chinese settlers, who were also a tough lot, for such the hard land demanded. A generalized quarrel over water rights finally came down to a fight between Koreans and Chinese over a single irrigation ditch in the summer of 1931. Though no one was killed, anti-Chinese feeling flamed in Korea, gleefully encouraged by Tokyo. The Japanese also revived another grievance. A Japanese army officer had been shot by Chinese soldiers in the hinterland of Manchuria in June, 1931, and the Japanese asserted that the authorities were not making strong efforts to discipline the culprits.

The punishment the Japanese inflicted was somewhat out of proportion to the crimes the Chinese had committed—even by Tokyo's standards. On the night of September 18th, 1931, Japanese troops seized Mukden, the key railway junction of Manchuria, which was a major industrial city as well. The sudden action was explained not merely as punishment for Chinese misdeeds. The Japanese said they had also discovered a plot to blow up sections of their South Manchurian Railroad. They had, they declared, acted to forestall the sabotage.

Their subsequent actions went far beyond either punishment or precautions. Within a few weeks, the Japanese Army had occupied major cities throughout Manchuria, meeting little resistance from the demoralized troops of the Young Marshal. Chang was himself in Peking, and his troops had little heart for a single-handed fight against greatly superior Japanese forces. By early 1932, the Japanese had taken over the three northeastern provinces of China in all but name. They organized an "independent" government and called the area

Manchukuo, the Land of the Manchus. To underline
the new "sovereign" status of Manchuria, the Japanese
found a chief of state out of the past. In March, 1932,
Henry Pu Yi, who had been the last Emperor of the
Manchu Dynasty, became Regent of Manchukuo. It was,
after all, the land of his great-great-great-grandfathers,
and the Japanese promised to protect his new kingdom
against the Chinese. He was, of course, an obvious puppet, for he could not take a single step without consulting his Japanese "advisers." All his actions were dictated
from Tokyo.

The Chinese did not meekly surrender, though they
were badly outclassed. The Japanese were harried by irregulars and guerrillas, as well as by the remaining
troops of the Young Marshal. Although they claimed to
rule Manchukuo—through Pu Yi, of course—without
opposition, the Japanese used the raids from south of the
Great Wall as an excuse for enlarging their conquests. In
January, 1933, Japanese and puppet troops invaded the
province of Jehol, a supply base for the weak Manchurian resistance forces. Jehol, they claimed, was really
part of Manchuria. In April, 1933, the Japanese began
moving south of the Great Wall which had, for centuries,
marked the northern boundary of China proper.

The Chinese response had been a series of diplomatic
compromises and a commercial boycott which truly hurt
the Japanese, who needed the profits of the China trade.
Although both Chiang Kai-shek and the Young Marshal
Chang had suffered personal humiliation through the
Japanese conquests, Nanking seemed incapable of effective military resistance. The Japanese had, after all,
moved into Shanghai itself, 2,000 miles from Mukden, in
early 1932 to crush the "boycott associations" centered
there. The 19th Route Army put up a stiff and brave
resistance against superior Japanese power. But the Jap-

anese were hampered chiefly by worldwide interest in the Shanghai struggle. It was one thing to maneuver in the hinterlands of remote Manchuria, but quite another to conduct major raids against helpless civilians in the most cosmopolitan city in Asia. Although the fighting ceased after three months, the Japanese had made their point. They could, it appeared plain, move troops without fearing truly effective resistance almost anywhere in China.

The attention drawn to China's plight by the "Shanghai Incident" finally forced the other powers to interest themselves in a settlement. An earlier suggestion that the Japanese be curbed had been tossed aside.

American Secretary of War Henry L. Stimson had demanded stern measures against the Japanese, including military opposition if necessary, when the "Manchurian Incident" began in 1931. But he had been overruled. Timorous "practical" men said that, first, the United States had its own problems with the internal economic depression and, second, Manchuria was really no business of ours anyway. No one can tell, of course, what would have happened if men had acted differently at that crossroads in history. An early check to Japanese ambitions *might* have avoided the bloody engagements of World War II in the Pacific when Japanese and American economic and political interests finally came into irreconcilable opposition. But no one can say what *would* have happened if Washington had behaved more courageously. Historians can only guess.

However, there can be no question that Japan was encouraged to seek greater conquests by other nations' failure to act. Even the settlement finally negotiated by the weak League of Nations gave the Japanese a great advantage. If it had not, the Japanese would not have agreed. The truce agreement of May 31st, 1933, provided that

Chinese troops would withdraw from a 50-mile-wide strip of land between Peking and the Great Wall. The Japanese also agreed to respect the "demilitarized zone," though that term was not yet fashionable. The settlement was patently unequal. The Chinese withdrew from territory, not even in Manchuria, which protected their ancient capital, while the Japanese were, in effect, given a free hand in Manchuria. The state of Manchukuo was not formally recognized, but the Japanese could act as if they controlled the entire area by law—as they did in fact. Beyond accepting the humiliation of creating a buffer zone—a kind of no man's land—on the soil of China proper, Nanking thus further agreed to give away a large and valuable area which had been Chinese for more than ten centuries.

Shortly after agreeing to a surrender which was scarcely veiled, Chiang Kai-shek faced a rebellion within his own Nationalist ranks. The leaders of the 19th Route Army, which had so staunchly defended Shanghai, were southern warlords with whom Chiang had already clashed. They were infuriated by the terms of the settlement. In November, 1933, the 19th Route Army occupied Foochow, the capital of Fukien Province, and proclaimed its own "People's Government." The leaders were by no means Communists. They were, however, for the moment in sympathy with the Communists, whose propaganda stressed the patriotic theme of resisting the Japanese. On the day after the formal proclamation of the "People's Government of China" in Foochow, the Government of the Soviet Republic of China and the Chinese Peasants' and Workers' Red Army signed an "Anti-Japanese Cease-Fire Agreement" with the Fukien regime and the 19th Route Army.

It appeared briefly that the Communists, creating a new United Front with a Nationalist group, were once more on the high road to power. That impression was reinforced when the Communist Central Committee convened at Juichin, the capital of Mao Tse-tung's Kiangsi First Soviet Area, in January, 1934. One weak Secretary-General was exchanged for another equally weak, while later-president of the People's Republic, Liu Shao-ch'i, became chairman of the All-China Labor Federation. He was to use that position and the labor unions themselves as a cover for subversion in the Kuomintang-controlled area.

Later the same month, there was a second meeting in Juichin. Mao called a session of the Congress of Soviet Representatives, the body that held real power. After re-electing Mao as chairman, the Congress affirmed a number of "laws" which approved the tactics Mao was using to win over the peasants. The two Communist meetings also promised support to the Foochow People's Government against the Japanese and Chiang Kai-shek. But the illusion of progress was short-lived. Even while the two bodies were meeting, the Foochow "People's Government" collapsed under Chiang's attacks. By October of 1934, the year that had begun so auspiciously, the Red Army and the Soviet Government were forced to evacuate the Kiangsi Soviet Area. The fabled Long March had begun.

Chiang's attention had been urgently directed to the Kiangsi Soviet by Mao's great success in winning the loyalty of the peasants and building strong armed forces. On the small stage of the isolated Kiangsi area, Mao used the same methods to create a power base he was later to use so successfully on the much larger stage of the Communist-controlled Border Areas in the northwest. Those areas were the launching pad for his final conquest of China. The blend of persuasion and benevolence with terror and brutality, all magnified by skillful propaganda

—as first tested in Kiangsi—was perfected in the Northwest. Beyond the Communists' inspired armed forces
and the Nationalists' dissension-ridden inefficiency, one
simple formula gave the Communists control of China.
Mao's manner of approach to the "working and peasant
masses" won him the support of the common people,
who were "China's chief natural resource"—and his own
chief source of power.

The nature of the Chinese people and their way of life
determined the Communists' techniques—and insured
their success. For almost a hundred years, since the beginning of the Manchus' unsuccessful wars with the
West in 1839, there had been neither peace nor security
in China. The depredations of bandits were made worse
by natural calamities—floods, famines, and pestilence.
The exactions of landlords, moneylenders, and tax collectors were inflicted upon a people who were already
suffering severely because the land could not support a
population that had suddenly increased sharply. A gray
hopelessness dominated the dreary days of the ordinary
Chinese peasant, whose only purpose in life was survival
—his only hope that things would be better for his children. Mao, above all else, made that hope appear a reasonable possibility, rather than an illusion.

The Communists could do little about natural calamities, but they could do much about man-made suffering.
The local landlords had their land taken away for distri-
bution to the peasants, the transfer being accomplished
without excessive gentleness. The peasants began to feel
that they were indeed being given a better life. After all,
an additional bowl of rice a day was a great change for
them. They also knew the satisfaction and excitement of
taking their revenge upon the landlords, moneylenders,
and tax collectors who had for so long lived upon their

labor like leeches sucking the lifeblood of a hard-driven water buffalo. Above all, the farmers felt themselves once again men and women, rather than creatures little better than their own few miserable beasts of burden. A slight improvement in present conditions and a well-founded hope of greater improvement in the future gave the peasants a new sense of human dignity. Man is, after all, the only animal that lives even more in the future than he does in the present.

The techniques developed in the laboratory of the Kiangsi Soviet are easy to describe, though they were difficult to apply. Mao's success was not easily won, because he was dealing with that least reasonable and most difficult of all animals, the human being. His chief methods were: giving the land to the men and women who farmed that land; appealing particularly to women, who had always been an oppressed class in traditional Chinese society; allowing—and stimulating—the "masses" to belief in Communism by making them feel that they were deciding their own fate through popular councils; sending propagandists and troupes of actors throughout his areas to tell tales and present plays which entertained the peasants and at the same time drummed the new faith into their receptive hearts; forcing his troops to respect the persons, rights, and property of the common people, in contrast to the marauding which had almost always marked Chinese troops in the past—and still marked the Nationalist forces; appealing to patriotism against the Japanese threat, thus giving the people an enlarged personal dignity because they belonged to the great *Chinese* nation-race; and, with the skill of a surgeon using his scalpel, conducting campaigns of terror against "class enemies" like the landlords and officials of the old regime. The result was, in most cases, an overwhelming rush of loyalty to the Communists, though they did not, if they judged it necessary, hesitate to use violence against the peasants themselves.

Mao's obvious success forced Chiang to seek his destruction. The Soviet Areas could no longer be regarded as a mere nuisance. They were, Nanking finally recognized, a major long-term threat to the existence of the Nationalist regime—and an immediately insurmountable obstacle to the consolidation of Nationalist power over China.

The first of the Five Extermination* Campaigns was, as we have seen, mounted as early as the winter of 1930. It had ended in Nationalist defeat, as, indeed, did all the Extermination Campaigns, except the critical Fifth—and last. Eleven divisions, numbering more than 100,000 men, attempted to encircle the Kiangsi Soviet, while smaller units struck at the smaller Soviets. Because they were contemptuous of the Communists, the Nationalists scattered their forces in Kiangsi, dividing them into two thin-pronged pincers and scattering them over large areas. Almost at their leisure, the Communists under Generalissimo Chu Teh concentrated their forces and broke first one claw of the pincers and then the other. The Nationalist commanding general was captured in the final battle of the five-day campaign which also gave the Communists 10,000 captives with 6,000 rifles. He imperiously demanded that he be told the amount of his ransom, for buying back high-ranking prisoners was a common practice in Chinese wars. Instead, he was tried by a "People's Court" and shot.

The pattern had been established. The Second Extermination Campaign was no more successful than the first, though the Nationalists used 200,000 men supported by 200 heavy field guns and 100 airplanes. The

* Also known as Annihilation or Encirclement Campaigns.

strategy was plotted by Chiang's German advisers. The campaign, beginning in February, 1931, did not end until May, 1931, but the Communists once again triumphed over Nationalist troops whose chief purpose was not to conquer, but to survive. The Red Army took 20,000 armed prisoners and added ten additional counties to the Kiangsi Soviet Area. The results of the first two Extermination Campaigns, the Nationalists themselves admitted, were "not encouraging."

Harassed by a well-founded feeling of insecurity, Chiang ordered the Third Extermination Campaign just a month later, in June, 1931. He took command himself, and it appeared for a time that he would finally succeed in destroying the Communists. Facing an enemy ten times their number, the Communists defended themselves by "scorched-earth" tactics. Leaving destruction behind them so that the enemy could not live off the land, they would retreat until they enticed the Nationalists into unfamiliar territory and strained Nationalist supply lines by extending them over great distances. Nevertheless, Chiang's personal forces, the best of the Nationalist armies, were at the gates of Juichin, the Red capital, by September, 1931. Then came the Mukden Incident, the Japanese attack in Manchuria.

Although the Communists succeeded in preserving most of their forces intact, they were saved this time not by their own skill, but by Chiang's distraction. The Mukden Incident not only forced Chiang Kai-shek's temporary retirement, but later effected a reconciliation between him and Wang Ching-wei, the man Dr. Sun Yat-sen had chosen as his political heir. Harried by those major events, Chiang abandoned the Third Extermination Campaign.

The Fourth Extermination Campaign began in June, 1932. The Nationalists fought under the slogan: "Fear no bandits, but underestimate no bandits! Seek them out and destroy them!" Mao still wished to resist with guerrilla tactics, but he came down with malaria, giving control over strategy to later-Premier Chou En-lai. Chiang had mobilized a half million troops, and matters appeared desperate. Again Chiang's personal troops fought well, slicing down the Communist areas sharply. But, once again, the Nationalists made the fatal error of dispersing their troops. A series of strikes by well-equipped and well-disciplined Communist forces cracked the Nationalist armies and ended the Fourth Extermination Campaign in March, 1933, nine months after it had begun.

The Communists were becoming a major, immediate threat. Both their numbers and the areas under their control had swollen as a result of the Extermination Campaigns, for each success brought them new adherents, including defecting Kuomintang regiments. Chiang Kai-shek, therefore, mobilized his full strength.

The Fifth—and decisive—Extermination Campaign began in October, 1933, after painstaking preparations on both sides. Mao Tse-tung attempted to make his base more secure by relaxing pressure on the "rich peasants." Anyone who was not a landlord was welcomed into the Red ranks. Mao also tried to make his areas economically independent of the semi-secret trade they had always carried on with the "White Areas." Chiang Kai-shek, in his turn, mobilized the local gentry against the Communists, clamped an effective blockade on the Kiangsi Soviet, and organized special infiltration and espionage corps. The Fifth Extermination campaign was, thus, the first in which the Nationalists used political warfare—and it was successful.

Compelled as much by shortages of food and munitions as by military pressure, the Communists decided in early October, 1934, they must evacuate the Kiangsi Soviet Area. Thus began the Long March, the strategic withdrawal which was blessed by the Comintern in a telegram received at the end of October. By that time, the Communist forces had already been on the road for two weeks. They were truly snatching victory of a sort from defeat by preserving the hard core of their leadership and their armed forces.

CHAPTER 8

The Long March

THE COMMUNIST FIRST Front Army set out from the Kiangsi Soviet Area just three and a half weeks before Nationalist troops seized the capital of Juichin from the weak rear guard. If haste was essential, planning was inadequate for the great retreat which took an entire year and traversed 8,000 miles. The expedition which was to become *the* heroic epic of the Communist movement began with 30,000 troops fleeing Nationalist encirclement. They carried with them printing presses, gold, silver, paper banknotes, and sewing machines—but no adequate maps. Their original objective was the Soviet Area that General Ho Lung, one of the leaders of the Nanchang revolt, had set up around Sangchih in northwest Hunan Province, 650 miles from Juichin. There they hoped to find refuge and reestablish the dominant First Soviet Area under Mao Tse-tung.

But their route betrayed their plans to Chiang Kai-shek, who had, finally, learned how to cope with the

Communists—at least, militarily. When Ho Lung's Second Front Army began pushing outward in mid-November, 1934, the Nationalists threw an army corps between the converging Communist forces. Despite a victory on the banks of the Hsiang River in eastern Hunan, when the troops formed a double line to allow the non-combatants to pass through, Mao's First Front Army discovered that it would not cut through the Hunan. Instead, pressure on General Ho Lung's Second Front Army became so intense that he, too, was forced to evacuate his base.

The two chief Communist armies in eastern China could still outfight the raggle-taggle provincial troops. But they could not defeat the central government troops of Chiang Kai-shek, which not only outnumbered them, but were better equipped. There was, after all, a limit to what the inspired spirit of Communist dedication could accomplish, whatever Mao Tse-tung said.

The time had obviously come to obey a maxim of Mao which later became famous: "When the enemy retreats, we attack! When the enemy attacks, we retreat!" The enemy, flush with his previous victories, was attacking—and the Communists retreated. Almost without a conscious decision, they began to move toward the Soviet Area in northern Szechwan Province where Chang Kuo-t'ao was entrenched with his Fourth Front Army. Although Chang was Mao's chief rival for power within the Communist Party, his base on the edge of the isolated Szechwan Basin was the one secure refuge left to the defeated Communists.

But Mao was still the guiding spirit of the Communist movement in the midst of its mass migration, and Mao had two purposes. The first was to preserve the hard core of the Red Army as a nucleus for building a new and more powerful Red Army. The second was to establish

the absolute power of Mao Tse-tung over the Communist Party and the Red Army. The two purposes were
equally important in his mind, and he was, in time, to
achieve both.

Up to the beginning of the Long March, Mao Tse-
tung had gradually attained greater power, but he had
been far from dominating the Communist movement,
divided as it was geographically and politically. Indeed,
Mao's own character was fixed by the struggles—internal
and external—which led up to the Long March. From
the fall of 1934, however, the 41-year-old Communist
leader was a completed individual. He himself would
change little, but he would change the Communist
movement greatly.

Mao's name has recurred at every critical juncture of
the Communists' history. But the name Mao Tse-tung
has been, in a sense, just a convenient label. We have
been discussing a name, rather than a flesh-and-blood
human being, who was moved as much by his own com-
plicated character as he was by the ornate doctrines of
Marxism.

The questions remain: *Who*, in truth, was Mao Tse-
tung? *Why* did he finally come to dominate the Communist movement in China as strategist, theoretical thinker,
military leader, and dreamer of great dreams—as hardly
any single man has ever dominated another historical
movement of comparable magnitude?

Hindsight is always clearer than foresight. But Mao
Tse-tung, born the eldest son of a "rich farmer" of Hunan Province on December 26th, 1893, was almost, it
seems, from the moment of his birth trained by history
itself for the role he played. His family had enough
money to give him an education of sorts, for, without
education, he could never have risen to command Chinese Communism. But his newly prosperous family was

rooted in the soil, so that he knew intimately the peasants of China, who were almost 85 per cent of the population —and were the raw material from which he shaped his power. His father was a harsh and avaricious small trader. The older Mao early made his son feel a sense of guilt over the family's exploitation of the "masses." He also aroused great personal resentment by his strict discipline. Mao's youthful resentment of his father was later transformed into hatred of the "capitalists and imperialists" whom, he felt, his father served in his own petty way. His revenge was to be taken against the entire "bourgeois" class which gave him birth.

Besides, the times themselves made Mao Tse-tung a revolutionary. China, as Dr. Sun Yat-sen and others had so eloquently protested, was humiliated and exploited by foreign nations. Mao was eighteen before the Republic supplanted the Empire in 1911. His most impressionable decade passed between the Revolution and the establishment of the Communist Party in 1921, when he was not quite 28. It was a time of fearful confusion, when greedy warlords, backed by foreign firms and nations, fought for spoils upon the torn body of China. The idealism and resentfulness which are the natural gifts of youth were, therefore, developed to the highest degree in Mao Tse-tung—and, equally important, they were given a logical and precise direction: "Salvation of the Nation."

That purpose was to become the secular religion of the heavy-set young man with the unruly brush of black hair, whose body and mind alike moved slowly—but with immense determination—towards their set goals. He was always fond of the ladies. Some of his companions said he was excessively fond of them. He treated "female comrades" and "women of the masses" with a respect which was unusual even among the free-thinking Communists, who believed that the subjection of women was one of the worst aspects of traditional Chinese culture. That fondness for the ladies—and the intensity of his emotions—was to be demonstrated by his four marriages —and numerous love affairs. He was also a chain smoker. A lumpy, homemade cigarette perpetually hung from the full lips which, with the general mildness of his heavy features, gave his face a deceptively feminine cast. If he was always greatly attracted to women and had a curiously feminine streak in his own character, he also believed in his personal intuition as much as any woman. That intuition told him that he was chosen to lead the movement which would "Save the Nation."

His drive toward supreme power stemmed as much from his determination to justify his own erratic life as it did from his dedication to Marxism. He was, after all, a member of the class Karl Marx himself had called the *"lumpen* intelligentsia," young men who were but half-educated, unsettled in society, and without fixed purpose. Mao's education was spotty, and he never actually finished a single formal course of study, whether it was in a "modern" primary school that taught little more than the Confucian classics, a commercial and law "college," or a special "institute" of soap-making. His higher education was limited to the occasional classes he attended—and the conversations he enjoyed with students and professors—while he worked as a clerk in the library of Peking University, China's premier institution of higher learning. Nonetheless, Peking University made him first a socialist and then a Communist through its Marxist Study Club and the persuasion of professors like the Communist Party's first Secretary-General Ch'en Tu-hsiu.

Given his sporadic education, it was not remarkable that Mao's grasp of the complexities of Marxism remained rather weak. Not until 1937, when his power was firmly established, did he acquire a "political secretary" who was an authority on Marxism. That secretary taught Mao much and amplified the Marxist theory to support Mao's visionary ideas. Mao Tse-tung himself was always an emotional Communist, rather than an intellectual Marxist.

His one fixed creed, formed early, was his faith in the peasantry. That faith sustained him as the Long March pursued its weary way across the mountainous terrain of southern China, harassed primarily by provincial troops, which were more nuisance than threat. The Communists did not yet know quite where they were going in December, 1934, as they entered the mountains of Kweichow Province in the far south. But they still moved so fast that the cumbersome military machine of the Central Government, which depended upon weight of men and guns rather than rapid maneuver, could not catch them.

Slicing through the disorganized provincial forces, which preferred not to fight, the First Front Army took Liping in eastern Kweichow Province in late December, 1934. A meeting of the Political Bureau members present decided tentatively to press on into Szechwan 300 miles away to join Chang Kuo-t'ao's Fourth Front Army. But a major engagement intervened—and altered the course of Chinese history.

On New Year's Day, 1935, the First Army Group under General Lin Piao crossed the Crow River after a brief skirmish and, a week later, occupied the central Kweichow city called Tsünyi. Taken by surprise, the local forces had retreated without firing a shot, but the local commander managed to rally them for an orderly retreat southward. On his enforced journey, he met two divisions under Nationalist General Wu Chih-hui marching north along the railroad from Kweiyang, the provincial capital. General Wu quickened his northward pace, intending to attack Tsünyi before the Communists could consolidate their positions. But he was assuming that the Communists were hampered by slow and uncertain tactics as he was. Actually, the Communists had no need for elaborate preparations because they were always ready to fight. Besides, the Communists were too clever to be trapped into the positional warfare General Wu Chih-hui envisioned. Instead, the Nationalists ran into a blocking force set up by General P'eng Teh-huai's Third Army Group ten miles south of Tsünyi. While Wu's troops were feeling out the enemy, Lin Piao's First Army Group swung wide to the east to catch them in the rear. The Kweichow forces were surrounded.

With just two regiments, General Wu broke through the Communist lines and fled toward the Crow River, sixteen miles to the south. He succeeded in getting away, for Communist troops in hot pursuit arrived at the bridge over the Crow to find that General Wu and his staff had already crossed, leaving most of their troops on the northern bank. Afraid that the Communists would follow up their advantage by taking Kweiyang itself, General Wu had dynamited the southern end of the bridge.

Almost 2,000 Nationalist troops were trapped on the northern bank of the Crow River, which was in that season almost 300 yards wide. They were marched back to the city of Tsünyi, where they fully expected to be shot. Instead, they were paid three Chinese dollars each for their rifles and were then given the choice of being released or joining the Communist forces. While Generalissimo Chu Teh himself harangued the officers, other Communist leaders spoke with the enlisted men. Finally, according to Communist reports, 80 per cent of the captured troops chose to join the Red Army, while the rest were given safe-conduct passes to their homes—and a small travel allowance.

The battle, gratifying as it was to Mao, was but the background to the critical Tsünyi Conference of senior Communist leaders which he hastily convened. The time had come, he felt, to grasp supreme power. Only a portion of the Central Committee was present—and those men all lay in his palm. Some objected that the Conference at Liping, a week earlier, had already decided all outstanding issues, but Mao insisted.

With military power firmly in his hands and his chief rivals far away, Mao Tse-tung made his bid for power. The first order of business was, however, the reorganization of the unwieldy Red Army. When Mao's men had been confirmed in commanding positions, he bitterly attacked the policies of the "Russian faction" and demanded that the Party choose a new Secretary-General. He was not himself named to the post, for the meeting chose Chang Wen-t'ien, a weak figure, who later unsuccessfully opposed Mao in the 1950s. Real power went to Mao Tse-tung, who was elected chairman of the Central Committee and the Political Bureau. He has been known as Chairman Mao ever since—and, until ten years after the establishment of the People's Republic, no one successfully disputed his power.

The Tsünyi Conference, held in a two-story mansion surrounded by broad balconies under a tiled roof, also gave the dispirited Red Army a new purpose expressed in the slogan: *Pei-shang K'ang Jih!*—Northward to oppose the Japanese! While the immediate objective was still Chang Kuo-t'ao's Szechwan Soviet Area, the soldiers were told that their final objective was the far northwest, where they would actively resist Japanese penetration of China. While reaffirming Mao's policy of "mobile war-

fare," the Conference thus invoked Chinese patriotism
to inspire the Red Army. The troops had been successful
in breaking out of the Nationalist encirclement, but they
had also taken heavy losses in the battles along the way.
They badly needed a new purpose. With the beginning
of the new year, Mao gave them that purpose—and confirmed his powerful personal influence over the common
soldiers of the Red Army.

The Communists' quick victory at Tsünyi had further
consequences. They were, perhaps, less far-reaching than
Mao's taking supreme power, but they were still highly
important. The Nationalists were dismayed by the Red
victory. General Headquarters issued new orders to its
own Central Government troops and to the Hunan,
Kweichow, and Szechwan provincial forces. Several divisions were withdrawn from their blocking positions in
northwest Hunan, where they had been gradually
squeezing Ho Lung's Second Front Army. The destruction of Mao's First Front Army, always the Nationalists'
primary purpose, became a matter of overwhelming
urgency. After the blockading divisions were withdrawn
to begin the fruitless pursuit of Mao Tse-tung across
southern China, Ho Lung broke out of his untenable
Hunan Soviet Area to begin his own little Long March
to the northwest. About forty thousand men were under
his command, a substantial reinforcement for the moving Communist forces. General Ho's Second Front Army
was also a major problem for Nationalist strategists, for
they had to deal with two separate main forces. Each
would split into independent columns when the tactical
situation made dispersion the best defense; they would
come together to attack when the enemy was weak.

Tales of the Long March have already filled several
books. Most have been produced by Chinese writers,
who deliberately romanticized the heroic retreat in order

to make it the great unifying legend of the Communist movement. Innumerable individual adventures enlivened the great adventure of one hundred thousand men trekking across China by a route that corresponds roughly to a hike across the United States from Kentucky to Oregon by way of Arizona.

One adventure that ended peacefully began when the vanguard of the First Front Army under one-eyed General Liu entered the mountains of southwestern Szechwan inhabited by tribespeople called Lolos. The Red Army feared it would have to cut its way through Lolo warriors armed with broadswords and long spears, for an unarmed work company had been stripped of its tools and clothing in their first encounter. The prospect was not inviting, since the terrain was unfamiliar and the troops were tired.

Although the Communists paid the "toll money" the Lolos demanded, the conclusion was still in doubt. Scenting further loot, the tribesmen refused to allow the Red troops to pass. Just as a fight appeared inevitable, an emissary of the Lolo chieftain galloped up. The Communist spokesman stressed that his followers were enemies of the provincial troops which regularly harried the Lolos. After an exchange of presents, General Liu and the Lolo chieftain swore eternal friendship by drinking the blood of a sacrificed cock. The Lolos then guided the Red vanguard through the mountains to the Szechwan army's outposts. The provincial troops welcomed the Reds as reinforcements, for they believed that the First Red Front Army was still hundreds of miles away. They were quickly disarmed.

Not all the encounters with native peoples ended as happily. After General Ho Lung joined his Second Front Army with Chu Teh's First Front Army on the edge of the Tibetan plateau in the late spring of 1935, fierce

Khampa horsemen constantly harassed them. Having moved his Fourth Front Army from the Szechwan Soviet Area to escape increasing Nationalist pressure, Chang Kuo-t'ao also camped on the windy plateau. The Khampas kept his forces in a virtual state of siege. "They would," he recalled, "throw a few shots into our camp and then follow up with a mad dash. Everything beyond our campfires' light was hostile. I was very glad to leave the Tibetans behind."

The decision to leave the Tibetans behind and advance to the northwest, where a small Soviet Area had already been established, was reached at a conference at Maoerhkai in western Szechwan in the early summer of 1935. All the contending leaders of the Communist Party were gathered together, except for the rear guard left behind in Kiangsi. Though Chang-Kuo't'ao made one more effort to unseat Mao by intimidating Chu Teh, he failed. The Maoerhkai Conference agreed that it must find a secure base—and Shensi Province in the northwest offered three advantages. It was remote from Nanking; the local Communists had already staked out a small area; and it was close to the Soviet Union. The Fourth Front Army, however, struck out even farther west when its leader, Chang Kuo-t'ao, came into open conflict with Mao Tse-tung.

The last stages of the Long March were probably the most arduous, though the enemy was nature rather than man. From the Tibetan border, the Red Army traversed the Great Snow Mountains and, finally, the seemingly endless prairies called the Great Grass Plain. Food was scarce, and the waving fields of grass grew from thick and nearly impassable mud swamps. Finally, however, the Red Army arrived in Shensi, an ancient province with a great history and a yellow, powdery soil called loess.

Songs blaring from Communist loudspeakers startled

birds whose remote ancestors had watched pioneer Chinese pilgrims making their way to India. Shensi and neighboring Kansu were the earliest sites of Chinese civilization, the cradle of empire. Shensi was itself the original principality of the feudal King of Ch'in, who unified China 220 years before the birth of Christ. Later, the founder of the most magnificent of Imperial dynasties, the T'ang, had cajoled his father into undertaking the conquest of China from the stronghold he ruled as governor of Shensi.

But the glory was long departed when the Red Army began to arrive in the autumn of 1935. The people were poor, and the soil was barren. Sian, the capital, was a dusty and impoverished provincial town, though it lay only a few miles from the ruins of the old Imperial capital, Changan. But Shensi was a refuge well suited to rebuilding the Communist military machine. In November, 1935, the Red Army took Yenan, a small community in a shallow bowl surrounded by hills pierced with cave dwellings. Yenan was to be the capital from which the Communists conquered China. There was to be no peace, but war to the end.

CHAPTER 9

The Alliance Remade

NOT SO MUCH a perverse sense of humor as a deliberate offering to fortune inspired the names of three cities in Shensi Province, where the Communists were the latest in a millennia-old line of armed settlers. The men who conquered China from the heart province had called their cities after the one thing they all said they desired. Besides Sian, the city called Western Peace, there had been Changan, the first Imperial capital, named Long Peace, and Yenan, Extended Peace, which the Communists first took and temporarily evacuated. Paoan, which means Ensured Peace, became the Red capital for about a year before the return to Yenan.

But there was no peace in 1936, any more than there had been peace in Shensi for thousands of years. The Communists extended their control over the sparsely settled plains of their northerly "Border Area" by armed power, not failing to "purify" their ranks by a purge of the local Communists who had welcomed them so joy-fully. At the same time, Japanese pressure on North China intensified. Although Shensi did not come under direct attack, neighboring provinces were infiltrated by Japanese troops. It was a three-sided small war, for Chiang Kai-shek concentrated his best forces against the Communists, rather than the Japanese.

The Communists' successes—and their failures, as well—often had the unfortunate consequence of attract-ing renewed Nationalist attention. The pattern had been set by Nationalist attacks against Ho Lung's previously secure Hunan Soviet Area when Mao's First Front Army began the Long March with a feint in his direction. Except for a handful of guerrillas in the hills, the Na-tionalists were left in virtual command of both the origi-nal Kiangsi Soviet and the Hunan Soviet Areas. The pat-tern had been repeated during the Communists' progress through Kweichow, Szechwan, and Yünnan. Chang Kuo-t'ao had, finally, been forced to evacuate his Szechwan Soviet Area, embarking on his independent Long March into far Kansu in the extreme northwest, his defiance insuring his later break with Mao Tse-tung—and the Communist Party.

In a number of provinces, Nationalist authority had, therefore, been strengthened by the Communist danger. The Nanking Government of Chiang Kai-shek had not brought those provinces under total control. But local commanders were frightened by the Communist menace and the demonstrated weakness of their own troops, com-pared to both the Red Army and Chiang's Central Gov-ernment forces. They, therefore, drew closer to Nanking. The same process was occurring in Shensi as the Red Army settled in the summer of 1935. Once again, the Nationalists were giving greater attention to an area under immediate Communist threat. The Nationalists invariably displayed their new interest in an area by sending more troops.

A strange combination had arisen in Shensi. The local commander Yang Hu-ch'eng, directing the Northwest Army, cooperated with the Northeast (meaning Manchurian) Army of Young Marshal Chang. Their primary mission, assigned by Nanking, was to check the Communists' growing strength on behalf of the Central Government. But their own inclinations ran in another direction.

Japanese aggression was threatening all North China. After driving the Manchurian troops from their homeland five years earlier and humiliating the Young Marshal, the Japanese were moving into China proper. Suiyüan Province immediately to the north of Shensi was under increasing pressure, while the Japanese had already penetrated Chahar to the northeast. Shamed by their expulsion from Manchuria, the Northeast Army troops were eager to prove themselves by fighting the Japanese. But Nanking still followed a devious policy of placating Tokyo with soft words and hard territorial concessions. The two armies in Shensi were ordered to attack the Communists rather than the Japanese, a mission the Young Marshal executed with even less success than enthusiasm in early 1936. Two offensives against the Red Army resulted in two notable defeats— and lost the Manchurian troops many prisoners.

The captives were released after being indoctrinated. The Communists were, after all, fighting to spread their ideas, rather than merely to kill their enemies; the route to victory for the outnumbered Red Army ran through the minds of men, rather than through military cemeteries. The simple Communist appeal was particularly effective among the disheartened and homesick Manchurians: "Form a united Anti-Japanese Front and win back Manchuria by arms! Chinese should not fight Chinese when the Motherland is endangered! Our common enemy is the Japanese!"

Mao knew the Nationalist troops were unhappy at fighting a grinding war of attrition against Communists who claimed to be fervent Chinese patriots. They wanted to fight the Japanese, rather than the elusive Red Army.

Not only the junior ranks, but the commanding officers were susceptible to patriotic propaganda. As early as January, 1936, the generals of the Red Army had written an open letter to the Manchurian Army troops proposing discussions to plan united resistance to the Japanese. In February, 1936, the Communists ordered an action that, at once, extended their control and enhanced their patriotic appeal. The Chinese Soviet Republic dispatched a column of troops across the Yellow River into the "model province" of Shansi, where the old warlord Yen Hsi-shan still ruled. The Communists' announced purpose was not conquest, but an alliance against the Japanese, since Tokyo's army was closing in on Shansi. In August, 1936, the Central Committee of the Chinese Communist Party formally told the Kuomintang that it wished to end the civil war in order to concentrate Chinese strength against the Japanese. Operating "underground" in Peking, Liu Shao-ch'i, later president of the People's Republic, and his chief lieutenant, P'eng Chen, later mayor of Peking, (who were both purged in the Cultural Revolution of 1966-1969) were forming a core of student propagandists. Their slogan was: "Unite to fight the Japanese!"

When Mao followed those moves with orders to his troops to avoid battle with the besieging Nationalist forces, the Young Marshal Chang was convinced that the Communists should be his allies, rather than his enemies.

Under pressure from his younger officers, Marshal
Chang began corresponding with Chou En-lai, then the
effective "Foreign Minister" of the Chinese Soviet Re-
public. Soon the commander of Chiang's Northwest
Army was also writing friendly letters to Chou. The
Young Marshal even invited Communist General Yeh
Chien-ying to Sian to advise him on improving the ef-
fectiveness of the Manchurian troops.

A virtual cease-fire prevailed in Shensi. Chang Hsüeh-
liang not only demanded of Nanking that he move to
Suiyüan Province to fight the Japanese, but was virtually
the ally and quartermaster of the Communists. The
Northwest Army, too, observed a truce in practice. Only
General Ho, personally loyal to Chiang Kai-shek, took
the offensive—and was roundly defeated. In December,
1936, the Communists firmly established their capital in
Yenan, where it was to remain for ten years. They had
reason to feel secure in their informal alliance with the
Manchurian and Nationalist troops who were supposed
to be blockading and attacking them.

The situation had deteriorated so severely that Chiang
Kai-shek himself flew to Sian on December 7th, 1936, to
revive the fight against the Communists. When the
Young Marshal pleaded for orders to march against the
Japanese, Chiang replied: "First destroy the Commu-
nists!" Through five days of negotiations, the stubborn
Generalissimo maintained the position summed up in
his overriding slogan: "Unification [by crushing the
Communists] before Resistance [to the Japanese]!"

Finally, the Young Marshal was convinced that he
could not sway Chiang Kai-shek by words. Ignoring
the Generalissimo's commands, he made common cause
with the Communists. On the evening of December
12th, 1936, the Nationalist Northwest Army joined the
Manchurian Army in revolt against their commander-in-

chief. While General Yang's troops surrounded Chiang's bodyguard, a Manchurian company marched on the spa ten miles from Sian where the Generalissimo was quartered. For five days, Chiang contemptuously rejected his subordinates' pleas that he declare himself the leader of united resistance to the Japanese. Oscillating between despair and righteous indignation, intensified by fear of his rivals' political intrigues in Nanking, the Generalissimo felt sure he was to be killed. Through the thin partition of his room, he heard the officers of his guard discussing his fate. They agreed that the Communists would insist upon his execution for his "crimes against the Chinese people."

Still the Generalissimo would not compromise. He was determined to die resolute, rather than yield to blackmail. It was a noble—if somewhat shortsighted—resolve, for his death would remove the one man who could effectively lead the country against the Japanese. Chiang Kai-shek knew that only he could bring jealous local warlords into a working alliance. The Communists felt the same way, and their intervention saved the Generalissimo.

On December 17th, 1936, Chou En-lai landed at Sian Airport. The Young Marshal's personal airplane had brought him from Yenan to confront Chiang Kai-shek. The two met for the first time since they had been respectively commander-in-chief and political commissar of the Revolutionary Army on the Northern Expedition. When the door opened to admit the man Chiang had not seen in ten years, he was convinced that he faced his executioner.

Chou En-lai removed the crushed cap from his close-cropped hair, and the shadow lifted from his olive face. The electric light illuminated his high cheekbones, his precise, heavy eyebrows, and his long, straight mouth.

"Mr. Chairman," he said, "I have come to sign the articles of betrothal for the remarriage of the Communist Party and the Kuomintang."

Chou En-lai had brought a detailed program of political and military reorganization for Chiang Kai-shek's consideration. The proposals, which were to be put into effect only after a year of haggling, and then only in part, were:

Nationalist actions: 1) ending the Civil War; 2) granting freedom of speech and assembly, accompanied by release of all political prisoners; 3) convening a joint National Congress to set new political policies; 4) forming an alliance of the Kuomintang and the Chinese Communist Party against the Japanese; and 5) instituting effective programs for the welfare of the common people.

Communist actions: 1) ending armed rebellion; 2) giving up claims to separate Soviet Governments and Red Armies; 3) making democratic reforms in Communist-controlled areas; and 4) promising to stop seizing the holdings of landlords.

Chiang finally agreed after lengthy discussions, which salved his dignity. He knew that neither he himself nor the Communists sincerely intended to carry out all the conditions. Tentative agreement came only after Madame Chiang, her influential brother, T. V. Soong, and their Australian adviser, W. H. Donald, had come to Sian to sustain Chiang Kai-shek—and only after long consultation with the Young Marshal and the Nationalist commanders on the spot.

Both sides saw major advantages in the new alliance. A China united, even only in name, was attractive to the Generalissimo. His acknowledgment as supreme leader by all Chinese, including even the Communists, would enable him to crush his opposition within the

Kuomintang, while extending his control over provincial warlords in preparation for the next round against the Communists. Mao Tse-tung, on his part, swore to subordinate every other pursuit to joint resistance to the Japanese. He did not promise flatly to abandon his fight for control of all China, but indicated that he would postpone that quest. He spared Chiang because he believed only Chiang Kai-shek could lead the coalition against the Japanese. Since the Communists' doctrines told them that "imperialism" was the most dangerous enemy of their revolution, they feared the Japanese more than they did the Nationalists. The Kuomintang and the Chinese Communist Party therefore agreed in principle to shelve their quarrel in order to fight against the common enemy. But both saw the new alliance as a temporary truce, rather than the final end of their rivalry.

On Christmas Day, 1936, Generalissimo Chiang returned to Nanking in Young Marshal Chang's personal plane. A dazzling display of political acrobatics followed. The Generalissimo tendered resignations and retracted them; he assumed new posts and abolished old posts; he commended some subordinates and dismissed others. The Young Marshal Chang was the ceremonial sacrifice. He had resigned with profuse apologies; he had been tried; he had been convicted of mutiny; he had been pardoned—and he had finally been placed under house arrest. (Never totally forgiven, he still lives under relaxed house arrest on Formosa.) When the dust settled in midsummer of 1937, the Nationalists appeared finally ready to fight the Japanese alongside the Communists.

The KMT-CCP *entente* was a long time building. Its launching was hastened by the Marco Polo Bridge Incident of July 7th, 1937, when Japanese soldiers clashed with Chinese forces outside Peking. In August, the Japanese attacked Shanghai—and open war began. The Na-

tionalists and the Communists, each with their own reservations, endorsed the original nine-point program
Chou En-lai had presented to Chiang Kai-shek in Sian.
The chief concessions were both more show than reality.
The Red Army was renamed the Eighth Route Army and
was placed under nominal Nationalist command. The
Communist-ruled territories were called Border Areas,
rather than Soviet Areas, and were nominally subordi-
nate to the Nanking Government. The Communists also
sent delegates to meet Nationalist representatives at
Lushan in Kiangsi. The war itself was going badly. The
Chinese had already begun to withdraw from North
China under Japanese attack.

In September, 1937, the Nationalists agreed to the
new arrangements. To bolster the facade of the United
Front, Chou En-lai was sent to Nanking to "participate"
in the Central Government. He became a member of the
presidium of the Kuomintang and, subsequently, vice-
chairman of the Political Training Board, the body
which virtually ruled China throughout the war. Communists and Nationalists worked together in outward
harmony in a number of bureaus, particularly after the
government was shifted from Nanking to Chungking in
westerly Szechwan Province to escape the Japanese
armies.

The first significant Chinese victory was won by Lin
Piao at P'inghsing Pass in Shansi. Fighting alongside Nationalist troops, Lin held his forces in reserve until his
nominal allies had broken under frontal attacks. He later
noted that the Nationalists lacked both effective tactics
and discipline. But Lin's troops, hidden on the slopes,
fell on the Japanese when they advanced into the steep
pass. P'inghsing Pass was not only Lin Piao's—and
China's—first major victory, but a psychological turning
point. Patriotic Chinese of all political opinions rejoiced

at his demonstration that Chinese troops *could* defeat the Japanese juggernaut. The Communists, in particular, rejoiced at the demonstration of their apparent superiority to the Nationalists, as well as the Japanese.

Mao concentrated on building up his political and military strength in the territories where he had been granted *carte blanche* by agreement with the Nationalists. He harried the Japanese, but gave his chief attention to creating a politico-military force to conquer China after the war. His chief rival, Chang Kuo-t'ao, was read out of the Communist Party for insisting that its first purpose should be to destroy the Japanese, rather than to save and increase its strength for the later showdown battle with the Nationalists—winner to take China.

The Nationalists were equally devious. Each party to the new alliance worked primarily toward the conquest of power rather than the defeat of Japan. While accepting the Communist mission in Chungking, Chiang Kai-shek was blockading the Communist areas and struggling against the Communist underground in the diminishing areas under Nationalist control. The Japanese, for their part, rapidly expanded the territory under their military occupation after taking Shanghai. Their most effective enemy was not the Chinese armed forces, though some troops fought bravely and well, but the vast expanse of China itself.

The Japanese received political assistance from that eternal dissenter, Wang Ching-wei, the man Dr. Sun Yat-sen had named his political heir. Opposed to both Chinese parties, Wang issued a manifesto from British Hong Kong in December, 1938, urging China to make peace by compromising with Japan. Evoking no response, he willingly lent himself to Japanese plans. Finally, Wang became chief of a government established in Nanking under Japanese control. Although he attracted some minor support, he had as little freedom of action as did "Emperor" Henry Pu Yi of Manchukuo. The last of the Manchus and the last of the true republicans who had overthrown him had become equally powerless Japanese puppets. Some deep moral probably could have been drawn from their common fate, but most of China was too busy to grieve over their plight.

While the Japanese advanced and the Nationalists retreated, the Communists extended their "underground" power. In March, 1938, they had established bases in northwestern Shansi to supplement their Shensi-Kansu-Ninghsia Border Area. In April, 1938, they set up another new base in Hopei, the home province in which Peking lies. In May, 1938, another "liberated area" came into existence on the borders of Hopei, Shantung, and Honan. While the Japanese armies advanced, leaving a political vacuum, the Communists stealthily infiltrated the areas behind the conventional front lines.

In May, 1938, the New Fourth Army, its core the remnants left behind by the Long March, proclaimed a "liberated area" in the southern part of Kiangsu Province, where both Shanghai and Nanking lie. The region under the New Fourth Army was quite different from the other new "liberated areas," for that army was powerful enough to create a Soviet government under another name. The New Fourth Army, initially, also received some supplies from the Nationalists. Things were going well for the Communists. In August, 1940, they consolidated much of the territory under their control into the Shansi-Hopei-Shantung-Honan Border Government. The CCP thus enjoyed effective—if stealthy—control over the peasantry of a good part of northeastern China. It was not surprising that the Kuomintang was alarmed.

Early in January, 1941, tension between the nominal

allies erupted into a small war. Accounts of the circumstances that produced the clashes vary, each side claiming that the other was at fault. The result was, however, clear. Nationalist troops attacked the New Fourth Army, killing its commander and capturing its deputy commander, General Yeh T'ing, one of the original Nanchang rebels of August, 1928. The scattered remnants finally reunited under General Ch'en Yi, who had been the New Fourth Army's political commissar and was later to be Foreign Minister of the Communist People's Republic.

The KMT-CCP alliance had foundered as an effective vessel of policy. The appearance of unified action was, however, to be maintained for some time. But the war itself was about to undergo a radical change. On December 8th, 1941, by Chinese time, Japanese bombers attacked Pearl Harbor in the Hawaiian Islands. The United States thus became deeply involved in the Sino-Japanese War—and, unavoidably, in the KMT-CCP conflict. Americans were to be intimately concerned until the final Communist victory.

CHAPTER 10

Uncle Sam
or Uncle Sucker?

FROM THE COCKPIT of the scout bomber flaunting the glowing red balls on its wings over the somnolent American naval base at Pearl Harbor on the island of Oahu that Sunday morning, the exultant code words flew through the air to the gray aircraft carriers over the horizon.

"*Tora! Tora!*" (Tiger! Tiger!)

The Japanese admiral smiled his satisfaction. The attack on the American Pacific Fleet had begun. In less than two hours' time, the massively armored ships lay smoking and sinking along Battleship Row, their great 16-inch guns pointing crazily and impotently toward the suddenly silent skies from which destruction had fallen. The most daring—and most effective—single major air raid in history was complete. The Pacific Fleet, the greatest obstacle to Japanese plans, had been removed. The land and sea road to Southeast Asia lay open to the Japanese invasion armies and fleets.

The Japanese attack was a brilliant tactical success—and a spectacular strategic failure. Enmired in the morass of China and fearful of American intervention, Tokyo had decided to "take out" the fleet on which American power in the Pacific depended. Bogged down in China, the Japanese had decided to isolate their enormous opponent. They could not subdue China by force of arms, for the people were sullen, the terrain was inhospitable, and, upon occasion, Chinese armies harassed them successfully. Though the Japanese could always concentrate their forces to defeat mass attack, the Chinese, particularly the Communists, were uncooperative. They would not wait for the heavy, slow-moving counterattacks. It, therefore, appeared to Japanese strategists that the best way to solve the China Problem was to bypass the China Problem. Tokyo reckoned that the Chinese colossus, isolated by Japanese conquest of Southeast Asia, would finally collapse.

That fundamental strategic plan brought Tokyo into conflict with Washington as much as did the clash of Japanese and American economic and political interests in the Far East. Moved by a conviction of Manifest Destiny, the United States had been expanding into the Pacific Basin for three-quarters of a century. If the Atlantic was a British lake, the Pacific was obviously meant to be an American lake. Impelled equally by emotion, by economic interest, and by idealism, Washington had served notice on Japan that she must abandon her plans to conquer Southeast Asia—and must begin to recede from China. The Japanese answer was—Pearl Harbor.

The war that began with the single most effective use of airpower in history was to be decided by airpower. Moving under the umbrella provided by their land- and sea-based air fleets, the Japanese took almost all Southeast Asia in the six months following their attack on

Pearl Harbor. But the incredibly productive American industrial machine soon began turning out airplanes and carriers of ever-higher quality in ever-increasing numbers. Severely hampered by their scanty industry and their lack of raw materials, the Japanese were gradually ground down in the Pacific and were forced to disgorge most of their conquests. The great, decisive battles were fought at sea, chiefly by fleets of aircraft carriers that never saw each other. With the gradual erosion of Japanese power elsewhere, conditions in the China Theater inevitably began to improve. Yet the Japanese land forces were still powerful enough in the fall of 1944 to mount a major offensive against the air bases in southern China from which American bombers had been attacking supply routes and the home islands of the Japanese Empire.

Their own obsession with airpower was to prove as disastrous to the Nationalists as their inability to unite— and the desire of some of their leaders to make fortunes from the war. China could, up to a point, be defended by airpower, sustained by the popular will to fight the Japanese. China could not, however, be conquered by airpower, for only ground troops enjoying popular support could perform that feat. But the Nationalists chose airpower as the decisive element in the civil war they knew would follow the Allied victory.

As the war in the Pacific mounted in intensity, the war in China more and more became a contest between Nationalists and Communists for post-war political control of the nation. Handcuffed by their neo-Confucian, aristocratic approach to government, the Nationalists had neither built a base of popular support nor united their groups of semi-independent, semi-feudal warlords. Probably, they would have lost even if they had not placed their faith in airpower. By betting all their stake that

they could reconquer China from the air, the Nationalists insured their defeat. While Chungking played with
its shiny new toys, Yenan patiently built up its conventional ground armies and spread its "underground" political control of large areas under Japanese occupation.
The New Fourth Army Incident of January, 1941, had
effectively ended the strained KMT-CCP alliance against
Japan, though the outward form was maintained for several years.

American action in the China Theater against Japan
inevitably affected the *real* war fought between Nationalists and Communists. Like it or not, Washington was
embroiled in Chinese politics, particularly in the Kuomintang's internal skirmishing. American intervention
grew so complex that it became the subject of many
books, including the monumental *White Paper on Relations with China* issued by the State Department in 1949.
We can here only attempt a broad sketch of the American role in the continuing Chinese revolution while the
war against Japan was still being fought. The subject is
so complex that the final verdict has not—even after
more than a quarter of a century—yet been pronounced.

Nonetheless, the attitudes of two American generals
exemplified Washington's divergent approaches to the
perplexing problem. One was Commander-in-Chief General Joseph W. Stilwell. Among his other positions, he
was chief-of-staff of *all* the Chinese armies under Generalissimo Chiang Kai-shek. Both titles meant much less
than they appeared. The second was Major-General
Claire L. Chennault, commander of the U.S. 14th Air
Force, a valued "friend of China" and an intimate of the
KMT leaders. His obsession with airpower was, in part,
responsible for the Nationalists' loss of China. Chennault
was a great fighting soldier and a genius in fighter tactics,
but he was neither a strategic nor a political thinker. The

final effect of his great influence was harmful to Nationalist interests.

Yet Chennault was originally hailed as the man who
saved China. He put new life into the Chinese Nationalists and convinced them that they could successfully resist the Japanese. His tool was the obsolescent P-41
fighter, and his workmen were a mixed and colorful
cohort of American soldiers of fortune. Most of them had
been discharged from the United States Army and Navy
Air Corps before Pearl Harbor to fight as "civilians" in
Chennault's American Volunteer Group.

The Chinese called them Flying Tigers because of the
grinning, big-fanged tiger-heads painted on the long
cowlings of their fighter planes. They came from all over
the United States; they were drawn almost as much by
the romantic desire to fight against aggression as by the
great monetary rewards they were offered. General
Chennault had himself been retired as a major from the
Army Air Corps because of deafness. He was preaching
his revolutionary fighter tactics in vain when he was discovered in 1937 by Madame Chiang Kai-shek, the
Wellesley-educated daughter of the wealthy Soong family and sister of Madame Sun Yat-sen. He was totally ob-
sessed by his message. Chennault believed that airpower,
particularly fighters, was the single answer to China's
chief problem: How to oppose the technologically superior Japanese? Chennault provided a brilliant answer,
but the decisive battles were still fought on the ground.

The American Volunteer Group, incorporated after
Pearl Harbor into the U.S. Army, fought brilliantly.
Chennault taught his unruly pilots that a fighter aircraft
was, above all, a flying gun-platform, rather than a vehi-
cle for individual heroics. The greater the concentration
of firepower, he demonstrated, the greater the likelihood

of victory. Chennault concentrated firepower by teaching the Flying Tigers to fight in formation, rather than seeking dogfights with individual Japanese airplanes. When the Japanese fighter force encountered the Tigers, they found themselves opposed by three-plane units, rather than by single planes. The dash of Chennault's volunteers, using his brilliantly simple tactics, decisively defeated the Japanese in the air.

Chennault's personal persuasiveness was greatly increased by his winning the Nationalists' first real triumphs against Japan. He became an irresistible force. When the U.S. entered the war, Chennault preached airpower on a broader scale. Bombers, he argued, could decide the issue in China. The heavy bombers of the 14th Air Force could not only harass Japanese bases and Japanese shipping carrying raw materials to the home factories or troops to the fighting fronts. The bombers could also break the Japanese armies on the ground, he maintained.

Chennault's was an enticingly straightforward—almost surgically clean—strategy. It appealed forcefully to the Nationalists' ingrained preference for simple formulae. It also appealed to an American high command that wished to commit as little as possible to a China Theater of Operations which it considered of third importance after the primary effort in Europe and the secondary campaign in the Pacific. It was war on the cheap. Success was guaranteed by Chennault's eloquence and certified by his absolute sincerity.

But the surgical solution was hampered by conflicting demands for scanty supplies—the age-old problems of generals on outlying fronts. Because China was virtually isolated, only a limited quantity of supplies could enter the country—by air "over the Hump" of the Himalayas or along the Ledo Road from northeast India. All supplies and reinforcements first had to make the long journey from the U.S. to Calcutta. Personalities also clashed. Even if General Stilwell, the ground commander, had been the most mild and conciliatory of generals he would have clashed with both Chennault and the Nationalists. Stilwell was, however, anything but mild. His temperament and his methods were even more abrasive than the assertive Chennault's.

Stilwell was chief-of-staff of the Chinese armies and, for all pratical purposes, their quartermaster-in-chief as well, since he controlled the flow of American equipment. He could not avoid becoming a key figure in Chinese politics—the contests of Nationalist cliques against each other—as well as in the undeclared war between Nationalists and Communists. He was not called "Vinegar Joe" without reason, and his peremptory commitment to getting things done clashed with the indirect Chinese approach.

The dedicated infantryman, the man who was called the foot soldiers' foot soldier, was, nevertheless, well qualified for his assignment. He was not only one of the U.S. Army's ranking generals, but spoke good Chinese and had written perceptive reports on Nationalist and Communist capabilities during his long tours as military attaché in China. Washington felt that it was not only selecting the best man for the delicate political, diplomatic, and military assignment by appointing Stilwell, but was also paying the Chinese a subtle compliment by sending them a man who had studied their language and culture. The Nationalists would have felt otherwise, even if Stilwell had been docile. The Chinese, quite simply, did not—and still do not—welcome a general, a diplomat, or even a correspondent who knows too much about them. They feel, in the first place, that he is likely to have fixed ideas, and they fear, in the second place, that he is not likely to be taken in by Chinese pretenses and pretensions.

Physically unattractive, blunt-spoken, dogmatic, and intent on winning the war, Stilwell was received with reservations in Chungking. The Generalissimo's agreement to his appointment to the ceremonial post of chief-of-staff of the Nationalist armed forces was obtained by extreme pressure from Washington. Shortly thereafter, Vinegar Joe began to offend the Chinese by his two overwhelming concerns: fighting the Japanese, in Burma as well as China; and building up efficient, modernized Chinese ground forces, rather than relying on airpower. Chungking planned to conserve its resources for the final battle against the Communists by letting the Americans cope with the Japanese. Though the Nationalists' was a hard-headed and not impractical view, it naturally aroused Stilwell's ire. Chungking was, further, enraptured of Claire Chennault's plan to defeat the Japanese from the air. That strategy would, coincidentally, conserve the Kuomintang's ground forces for the war against the Communists to determine who would rule China after the Japanese defeat.

Stilwell was entrapped not only in a maze of pride and cross-purposes, but in the internal feuds of the Kuomintang. Chiang Kai-shek had never reconciled all his nominal supporters to his supreme power, though he had begun to build a strong political and economic base before the war. But he had paid heavily for his small success. The Kuomintang was sharply divided into cliques with conflicting interests, while the provincial generals gave grudging and perfunctory obedience to Chungking only because of the common threat from the Japanese.

Moreover, many Chinese officials, brought up in insecurity, used the war to fatten their pocketbooks and guarantee their families' security.

Stilwell's insistence upon using ground troops to fight the Japanese not only ran counter to Chungking's basic interests, but interfered with the enrichment of Chinese officials. He also became locked in a bitter quarrel with Chennault over allocation of scarce supplies, although he was the Air Corps general's superior as commander-in-chief of all American troops in the China Theater.

Despite his problems, Stilwell pressed ahead and created a good Chinese army of 15 to 20 divisions, known as Y (for Yünnan) Force. He was assisted by such first-class Chinese generals as Ch'en Ch'eng, who had distinguished himself during the Extermination Campaigns and was later to be vice-president of the Republic of China, and Sun Li-jen, an alumnus of Purdue and the Virginia Military Institute, who was later chief-of-staff of the Nationalist Armed Forces on Formosa. But Stilwell could secure commitment of only a few divisions to battle in Burma, for most of Y Force was held in reserve to fight the Communists after the war. A substantial proportion of Chiang's other effective troops was blockading the Communist-ruled areas in North China.

The atmosphere was further fouled by Washington's attitude and Chungking's greed. President Franklin Delano Roosevelt was inclined to patronize the Chinese and exclude them from major allied deliberations, though they were officially one of the Big Five with the U.S.A., the U.S.S.R.., the U.K., and France. Feeling the slights keenly, Chungking could thus excuse its passivity against Japan—while demanding ever larger shipments of American gold to support the Nationalist currency, which was astronomically inflated.

Tension grew so high that Stilwell was finally recalled

to placate the Chinese. A junior lieutenant-general, Albert C. Wedemeyer, was given Stilwell's responsibilities in China in October, 1944. He was much more diplomatic and much more sympathetic to the authoritarian Chungking regime and its understandable fixation upon the Communist menace. But even Wedermeyer concluded that it was impossible to expect the Nationalist regime to survive unless it enacted major political, economic and military reforms. Such reforms the Generalissimo did not really wish to effect—even if he could have done so.

While the Nationalists were intriguing against each other and their American allies, the Communists were systematically building their rural bases—and their "underground" apparatus in Japanese-occupied areas. Since few Chinese supported the puppet regime of Wang Ching-wei and the Nationalists ignored the opportunity, the Communists had a free field for "underground" work. By 1945, they claimed to rule 70 million Chinese —and possessed large numbers of secret adherents in areas ruled by the Japanese and the Nationalists. The influential intellectuals, dismayed and disillusioned by the Nationalists' decay, were with the Communists almost to a man. Mao Tse-tung saw the approaching end of the war in the Pacific with great satisfaction, for he was well prepared to win the peace—by conquering China. His armies had never been stronger, numbering between five hundred and nine hundred thousand, and his propaganda had never been more effective.

The Communists had adroitly used the alliance against the Japanese for political maneuvering. On October 10th, 1944, the thirty-third anniversary of the revolution which created the Republic of China, Chou En-lai issued a report on his continuing negotiations with the Nationalists. It was a remarkable attack upon a nominal

ally. Chou castigated the Kuomintang for tyranny, corruption, and failure to cooperate with the Communists.
The Kuomintang's faults, he asserted, had made it impossible for the Chinese nation to offer effective resistance to Japanese aggression. He called for the creation
of a "truly representative" National Assembly which
would lay the foundations for a "coalition government."
That government would bring together the Nationalists,
the Communists, and the smaller parties of the right and
left. That appeal was the core of a new five-point proposal for a new political order in China.

The Communists used the appeal for a coalition to
rally public support and to entrap the Nationalists in a
government which would end with Communist rule of
China. Just half a year later, in April, 1945, Mao Tse-
tung published his treatise, *On Coalition Government*.
He hardly bothered to camouflage his strategy of creating a joint government which would give the Communists respectability and power—and, finally, enable them
to take all power.

Chou En-lai was himself the Communists' chief representative in the discussions with the Nationalists which
followed his statement. Eager to secure peace in China
after the war's end, the United States took a hand in the
game. The man assigned to reconcile two parties which
had been fighting for almost twenty-five years was the
American ambassador, silver-mustached Major-General
Patrick J. Hurley. He astonished the Communist leaders
when they met him at Yenan Airport on November 7th,
1944, by yelling a Choctaw war whoop. The Red leaders were amazed at the quaint ways of the mysterious
Occident.

Hurley was, however, delighted by the results of his
mission. Having already been told by the Russian dicta-
tor, Joseph Stalin, that the Chinese Communists were

not *really* Communists, he took their proposals most seriously. Flying back to Chungking with the Communists' five-point draft, he was deeply disappointed to discover that the Nationalists did not consider the document the answer to China's problems. Contrasting the Communists' five-point proposal and the Nationalists' later three-point counter-proposal demonstrates how far apart the two parties were in reality.

The Communists offered these terms: 1) KMT-CCP military cooperation to defeat the Japanese; 2) a reformed coalition government; 3) adherence to the Three Principles of Dr. Sun Yat-sen in order to promote progress, democracy, justice, and civil rights; 4) all anti-Japanese forces to obey the orders of the coalition government; and 5) all anti-Japanese political groups to be recognized as legal political parties, particularly the Communists and the splinter parties.

The Nationalists replied with their own conditions: 1) the Communist armies to be incorporated as equal members of the national armed forces, and the Communist Party to be declared legal; 2) the Communist Party, in turn, to place its armies under the command of the National Military Affairs Council, which would include some senior Communist officers; and 3) the Communist Party implicitly to renounce Communism by subscribing to the Nationalists' desire to base the government of China upon the Three People's Principles, subject only to the restrictions imposed by the demands of the war.

The two documents may superficially have appeared fairly close together—or, at least, looked like statements which could be the basis for further negotiations. Actually, they defined the irreconcilable differences between the KMT and the CCP. The Communists wanted, above all, to become active members of the central government to which they were theoretically subordinate; they also wanted legal freedom for their political activities. The Nationalists were willing to grant that legal status, but they would not take the Communists into the government. Coalition government was, of course, the Communists' essential demand, for a coalition was their master-plan for political victory.

The negotiations would continue for several years, as would renewed fighting. Only for a moment was the struggle between Mao and Chiang for control of China put aside in joint rejoicing over the surrender of Japan on August 14th, 1945. The real battle was, after all, just beginning.

CHAPTER 11

The Second Civil War

THE FINAL BATTLE for China began even before Japanese surrender was accepted on August 14th, 1945. It was initiated by orders from Nationalist chief-of-staff, General Ho Ying-ch'in, to the Japanese immediately after Radio Tokyo announced the Empire's unconditional surrender on August 10th. General Ho instructed Japanese generals to surrender their forces and, even more important, their weapons, only to the official commanders of the various Chinese war zones, all Kuomintang officers. He instructed the Communist Eighth Route Army to remain in position and refrain from taking Japanese surrenders. By those orders, General Ho began the Second Civil War.

General Ho's orders were farseeing and logical. The Communists had clearly stated that they had no intention of abandoning their struggle to conquer all China, despite their proposals for a coalition government. But the general's order was also highly provocative, not to say unfortunate. It gave the inherently antagonistic Communists a perfect excuse for immediate disobedience.

The Communists would, of course, have done as they wished—order or no order. But Ho's directive gave Mao the clear pretext he required. The Chairman declared: "This order shows that Chiang Kai-shek has declared a Civil War against the Chinese people." He immediately ordered his armies to fill the power vacuum, scooping up Japanese arms and enlisting puppet soldiers. The bald hostility displayed by General Ho gave Mao not only complete freedom of action, but a tremendous psychological advantage. Mao could put it to the Chinese people, especially the intellectuals who were the technical, managerial, and opinion-making class, that he was merely responding to the KMT's open demonstration of bad faith. He could make the same appeal to public opinion in the victorious Allied nations, for he had become almost as concerned with international opinion as with the attitude of the Chinese people themselves.

Thus began the climactic battle for China, which the Communists call the Second Civil War. The manner in which the four-year conflict began foreshadowed its development. The Communists would fight and subvert. They would also negotiate with the Nationalists when it suited their purpose. They called their strategy "fighting while negotiating," graphically expressed in Chinese as: *Ta, Ta! T'an! T'an!*—Fight awhile and talk awhile, then fight and talk again! That strategy, laying equal stress upon fighting and negotiating, was the key to the Communist victory.

Equally important was the concentrated propaganda offensive, which was almost as intense abroad as it was in China. Under Mao's astute leadership, the CCP had come of age in international politics. The Chinese set the pattern for domestic and international propaganda which the Communists later used so effectively in Vietnam. The CCP was assisted by foreign publicists—some wholly sincere, others its secret agents. It also established its own propaganda apparatus abroad, utilizing "foreign friends of the Chinese people" to make propaganda on the KMT's undeniable inefficiency and corruption.

In the United States, which was the most important propaganda target, a number of front organizations conveyed a bombastic but highly effective message, which was sustained by truth, half-truths, and outright lies: "The Kuomintang is an evil, graft-ridden, faction-riven, and unpatriotic organization dedicated to the exploitation of the Chinese people through a Fascist dictatorship on behalf of domestic and foreign imperialistic-bureaucratic capitalism. The Chinese Communists are, of course, Marxists, but their immediate program is the New Democracy, which will unite all patriotic elements of China in a common effort to improve the lot of the Chinese people. Communism and the dictatorship of the proletariat are a long way off!"

One of the chief front organizations in the United States was called the Committee for a Democratic Far Eastern Policy. Its chief interest, however, was, at that point, directed to China. The Committee was very effective, enrolling many honest and idealistic scholars and political figures who were manipulated by professional propagandists. The Committee depended equally upon lecturers, letters to newspapers, special articles, and books, its own magazine, *Spotlight on Asia*, and "conferences on Asian problems." Attending a "conference" sponsored by the Committee for a Democratic Far Eastern Policy in the midst of the Second Chinese Civil War was a revealing experience, which has grown even more enlightening and pertinent with the passage of the years. The tactics of Asian Communists seeking to impose their

totalitarian rule do not change much. Neither, unfortunately, does the gullibility of well-meaning Americans.

Meeting in the plush ballroom of a major New York
hotel, the Committee attracted an audience of more than
five hundred, ranging from recognized authorities to
young students. The star of the performance was an
enormous Chinese general who spoke no English, but
sat with his immense hands resting on his broad thighs,
sagely nodding an enormous head covered with a stubble
of gray hair. He was the Christian General Feng Yü-
hsiang, who had fallen out with Chiang Kai-shek and had
been sent on a "study-tour" abroad. Such a tour was
standard procedure for dealing with difficult warlords.
General Feng was still playing the same tortuous game in
which he had so successfully competed in the 1920s and
1930s. This time, however, he was sporting with quite
another playmate, the Communists. The New York appearance was one of his last. On his way back to China
by way of the Soviet Union, he was killed in an "acci-
dental fire" on board a Russian steamer in the Black Sea.

Among the eloquent speakers at the "conference"
were: American labor leaders and businessmen who
knew nothing of China but movingly discussed the suffering of the Chinese people; scholars who went along
because they believed the Communists offered the only
hope for China; and some publicists who were later to
acknowledge their primary loyalty by openly accepting
employment under the Communists in China. The total
impact was overwhelming on young students who knew
little of China. Because the speakers could, quite hon-
estly, wax so righteously indignant about the faults of the
Kuomintang, few among the audience saw the flaws of
omission in their broadly drawn pictures of the heaven
on earth the Communists had created in the "liberated

areas"—and would subsequently create throughout China.

One came away glowing with sympathy for the earnest Communists, who had so often sought in vain to make peace with the treacherous Nationalists. One felt that the Communists primarily desired not power, but only the well-being of the Chinese people. Faint doubts as to the qualifications and loyalties of some speakers were submerged in the flood of eloquence which rolled over the red-and-gold ballroom—and was duly reported in the American press.

By pretending to be an impartial body concerned only with the welfare of China and the United States, the Committee for a Democratic Far Eastern Policy brilliantly achieved its purposes. Its mission was to prevent American assistance to the Nationalists by swaying American public opinion. The mission was executed so well by the Committee for a Democratic Far Eastern Policy and other organizations that the Nationalists never had a chance in the United States. It is, of course, unlikely that they would have had a real chance of victory in China even if the United States had intervened. But swinging American public opinion against Chiang Kai-shek was a telling blow.

While the babel of propaganda swelled as accompaniment to the in-fighting of negotiations in China, the CCP and the KMT were also moving troops. As soon as the Japanese surrendered, General Ho's orders and Chairman Mao's reply had set off a series of maneuvers and battles.

General Ho's 120th Division of more than 100,000 men moved rapidly from its base in Suiyüan to control railway lines and territory throughout the provinces of Suiyüan and Shansi. Other units, under General Nieh

Jung-chen, later chief of China's nuclear development, took Chahar Province and encircled the strategic triangle formed by Paoting, a major power center; Tientsin, North China's chief port; and Peking, the capital—all in Hopei Province. At the same time, the troops of one-eyed General Liu moved south into Honan Province, seizing railroads and control of the population. Other units took Shantung. The New Fourth Army, reformed under General Ch'en Yi, later Foreign Minister of the People's Republic, moved north to assert Communist rule in the decisive Central China region between the Huai and the Yangtze Rivers. By October, 1945, the Communists had expanded their territory from the 116 counties they held in China proper on V-J Day to 313 counties—and they were still on the move.

It would be tedious to attempt to describe in detail Communist and Nationalist military maneuvers during the four years of the Second Civil War. But it also is impossible to pass over the forced marches and the shifting battles, shaped by international political intrigue, which gave the Communists control of Manchuria. Just as the Manchus in the early 17th Century and the Japanese in the early 1930s had used Manchuria as a base for the conquest of China proper, the Communist armies would storm out of the Manchurian fastnesses to destroy the Nationalist regime.

The man assigned to take Manchuria was General Lin Piao, just 37 years old in 1945, but already hailed as the CCP's most brilliant field commander. In carrying out his assignment he was to become involved in a complex intra-Party struggle, which would have its final repercussions years later in the purges of the Great Proletarian Cultural Revolution. He was to enjoy the tacit support of the Soviet Armies of the Far East, which had marched into Manchuria in the closing days of World War II, and he was to have his minor differences with the Soviets. He was to engage in apparently endless—and usually fruit-less—negotiations with the Nationalists under the aegis of American Truce Teams. But he was, in the end, to consolidate Manchuria, build a formidable army, and launch that army into China proper.

Lin Piao started by drawing troops from other commanders to increase the strength of his own 115th Division. His troops, numbering more than 100,000, made a forced march to Manchuria, where they not only acquired vast stocks of arms and munitions from the surrendered Japanese Kwantung Army, but took in more than 75,000 puppet troops to increase their number to about 200,000. Aided by the Russians, Lin Piao was well on his way to building the single most formidable military force in China. He called it the Manchurian People's Revolutionary Army, for the Communists wished to present the facade of a united "popular front" against the Nationalists.

But the Russians, having entered the Pacific War belatedly in return for major concessions from the United States, were looking after their own national interests with even greater vigor than they were minding the interests of the CCP. They seized the naval bases of Port Arthur and Dairen, which they had held until the Japanese conquered them in 1905. They began dismantling major sections of the industrial plant the Japanese had built up in Manchuria, and trains along the Chinese Eastern Railway carried great packing cases to the junction with the Trans-Siberian Railway—and thence to the Soviet Union. What the Russians did not take, they destroyed. The total value of their loot—and destruction—from Manchuria is estimated at two billion dollars. Nor were the Russians quite ready to give unreserved support to a Chinese Communist movement which had proved disturbingly independent. They scrupulously maintained diplomatic relations with the Nationalist Government, which had returned to Nanking shortly after V-J Day, and they wrung major territorial concessions from that government.

At the same time, the United States was assisting the Nationalists—with reservations. Rebuffed when he asked the Soviet Russian commander in Manchuria for permission to send troop ships to Dairen, Chiang turned to the United States. American airplanes landed hundreds of thousands of Nationalist troops in Manchurian cities, while American ships transported other divisions to North China. The total air and sea lift had moved almost half a million soldiers by October, 1945. At the same time, U.S. Marines took up defensive positions in Shantung and along key railway routes in North China.

The pieces were arrayed on the board, and the chess game began. The only rules were stealth, deceit, and force. The political map of China looked like a series of interlinked ink blots. Manchuria was largely red. The chief cities of Manchuria were, however, Nationalist white, linked by white railway lines across which the red streaks of Communist harassment spilled. North and Central China were primarily white, with large red blots where the Communists had established "liberated areas." The game was hardly a simple, two-handed affair. The United States was playing a major role throughout China, while the Soviet Union still held the upper hand in Manchuria.

American assistance was, from the beginning, limited by several factors. There was much purposeful agitation in the United States to "stay out of Chinese affairs" and "bring the boys home," while Washington was reluctant to become too deeply involved. The limited intervention proved worse than no intervention at all. Unable to decide exactly what it wanted in China, the U.S. tried to achieve its ends largely by economic means. Bank loans bolstered Nationalist currency, while direct aid amounted to about one billion dollars for civilian relief and economic reconstruction, administered largely through the United Nations Relief and Rehabilitation Agency. Shanghai became again what it had once been: the most exciting city in China and a happy hunting ground for adventurers of all kinds.

But intermittent fighting flared in the countryside, and the United States tried again to reconcile the two parties. On November 27th, 1945, President Harry S. Truman appointed General of the Army George C. Marshall his "special envoy" to bring peace to China. In December, 1945, Truman announced the basis of his China policy: 1) cessation of fighting; 2) no American military intervention; 3) a nationwide conference of all parties to unify the country and create a government representing all elements; and 4) pledges of increased economic aid for national reconstruction. It was a noble program, but, unfortunately, it bore no relationship to the realities of a country where both Communists and Natinalists were determined to seize all power.

General Marshall's mission, undertaken in all sincerity, was to last until January, 1947, when he was withdrawn and the United States virtually washed its hands of China. For a little more than a year, Marshall had managed to keep the CCP and the KMT talking—and only fighting occasionally. His roving Truce Teams were effective only when it suited the purposes of the opposing local commanders, while his Executive Headquarters in Peking was known to the cynical Chinese as the Temple of the Thousand Sleeping Colonels.

Marshall's mission to China almost broke the heart of the great soldier and statesman. It did not, however, teach the United States that American moral standards and the American desire for peaceful solutions could not effectively begin to dissolve the ambitions, jealousies, and bitterness of decades which dominated China—and other foreign nations. Nor did it teach Washington that American intervention in a crisis abroad could only be successful when the United States was prepared to back its policy with appropriate force. Finally, the Marshall Mission failed to drive home the lesson that good intentions count for little in the bloody arena of international politics.

Marshall did succeed in wringing apparent limited agreement from the CCP and the KMT on local cease-fires and nationwide political conferences. Mao Tse-tung had, after all, flown to Chungking to confer with Chiang Kai-shek soon after the war ended, their first meeting since the Northern Expedition had begun in June, 1926. But both sides seized every opportunity to extend the territory under their control by military means. Even assuming good faith in the negotiations, which was a large assumption indeed, it soon became clear that the objectives of the two sides were irreconcilable. The Nationalists were willing to grant the Communists participation in nationwide deliberative bodies which had no power. The Communists would settle for nothing less than coalition government, a device which would, in time, give them all power.

Fighting continued in Manchuria, with the KMT holding an apparent advantage. The Communists were, however, following their familiar strategy of building up their strength in the countryside—not only in Manchuria, but throughout China. Shortly after Marshall left China, the civil war broke out again with doubled violence.

Although the Nationalists took Yenan, the Communist

capital, on March 19th, 1947, the CCP had prepared for that eventuality. For the first time since the "adventuristic" Li Li-san Line had held sway over the Party's policies in the late 1920s, the Communists were ready to move from the countryside against the cities, where real power lay. Mao ordered the newly named People's Liberation Army to "take the cities, after having encircled them from the countryside." In December, 1947, the Chairman formally recognized the situation which had developed during the preceding year by proclaiming: "The Chinese people's war of liberation has become an offensive on all fronts."

The United States had attempted to force the Kuomintang to reform, first through the Marshall Mission and, later, through a second special mission headed by General Albert C. Wedemeyer. Rejecting the belief that only Chiang Kai-shek could lead the Nationalists to victory and unify China, the United States had placed its hopes in the indeterminate groups it called "liberals." But Washington had given no significant military, political, or economic aid to any leader other than Generalissimo Chiang Kai-shek. Instead, General Marshall had expressed a vague hope: "Successful action on their [the liberals'] part under the leadership of Generalissimo Chiang Kai-shek would, I believe, lead to unity through good government."

Mao Tse-tung, for his part, neither entertained vague hopes nor hesitated to make flat judgments. Failing to insure Nationalist victory, the half-hearted American intervention had confirmed Communist enmity. Mao told an American correspondent:

"Judging by the large amount of aid the United States is giving Chiang Kai-shek to enable him to wage civil war on an unprecedented scale, the policy of the U.S. Government is to use so-called mediation as a smokescreen for strengthening Chiang Kai-shek in every way and suppressing the democratic forces in China through Chiang Kai-shek's policy of slaughter so as to reduce China to a virtual U.S. colony."

The irresolute American policy had neither been effective nor won gratitude. It is unlikely that even full-scale American intervention and American imposition of major reforms on the KMT would have prevented the Communist victory. Certainly, partial intervention proved disastrous. All circumstances favored Communist victory.

CHAPTER 12

"The Chinese People Stand Erect!"

ONLY TWO YEARS elapsed between the time General George C. Marshall washed his hands of the Chinese mess in January, 1947, and the Communists' capture of Peking which insured their conquest of all China. Only eight months elapsed between the fall of Peking and the morning of October 1st, 1949, when Mao Tse-tung, standing in the Emperor's traditional place on Peking's Gate of Heavenly Peace, proclaimed the establishment of the People's Republic of China.

"Today," he declared, "the Chinese people stand erect!"

The Communists' was truly a popular victory. They were carried to triumph on the shoulders of the aroused Chinese people. From intellectuals to peasants, from small artisans to middle-rank capitalists, the Chinese people longed for peace and a stable government. Having despaired of the Kuomintang's fulfilling their hopes, they gave their loyalty to the Communists. They were

moved as much by disgust with the Nationalists' inefficiency and corruption as by confidence in the Communists' promises of a glowing future of material abundance
and social justice. Except for a few "war criminals" like
Chiang Kai-shek and his closest supporters, the Communists promised equal treatment to all Chinese under
the New Democracy.

Sheer Chinese patriotism also attracted great numbers
to the Communist cause, for the Communists sought
to make China a great power once again. Nor were they,
in the beginning, narrow-minded in their policies on
their recruiting. They were not only eager to accept Nationalist deserters *en masse*, but indiscriminately enlarged the Communist Party itself—from 1.2 million in
early 1945 to 4.5 million in October, 1949. The rapid expansion attracted support, as did the wooing of minority
parties like the Kuomintang Revolutionary League, the
Democratic League, and the Chinese People's Salvation
Association.

By strict Marxist standards it was impossible to expand
a Communist Party more than three-fold in five years. So
many new members could hardly be given the ideologi-
cal training or taught the absolute discipline which make
true Communists. But the CCP was concerned to achieve
power, rather than to preserve the purity of the Party.
There would be time after victory to purify the ranks,
just as there would be time to make the "allied democratic parties" into marionettes. In the meantime, the
hard core of the CCP remained intact—and undeceived
by talk of the New Democracy. Their creed allowed—
indeed, actually ordered—the use of lies, murder, and
terror to gain victory. After they had won the hearts and
minds of the people and thus taken control of China, the
Communists would have much time to conduct the necessary purges.

Popular support was just one of a number of forces that carried the Communists to their final victory over a dispirited and disunited Kuomintang. Like all successful guerrilla wars, the Chinese revolution was won by a combination of tactics. Demoralizing the enemy and winning popular support was a preliminary stage. Mao Tse-tung described the force which was decisive in the final struggle in two brief aphorisms: Power grows from the barrel of the gun! Without a people's army, the people have nothing! After years of preparation, the time had come to strike with powerful conventional military forces. The conquest of the centers of power by massed armies, fighting positional battles with superior firepower, was the last stage. Mao was, of course, right. Without the People's Liberation Army, he never could have conquered China.

Mao handled his expanding armies with all the dash and stealth he had learned in his years as a commander of guerrillas. The final campaigns were planned by Generalissimo Chu Teh and his highly professional staff officers, who had learned their trade in decades of unequal combat. The Red officers no longer avoided battle with the numerically superior KMT forces. But they still maneuvered to prevent the KMT's concentrating its forces for a decisive blow against massed Red troops.

Manchuria, where the Communists enjoyed great advantages, was to be the decisive battleground. Lin Piao's force, renamed the Manchurian Allied Liberation Army, had grown to a strength of more than 800,000 against the 500,000 motley troops the KMT mustered. Moreover, he held more territory, surrounding the KMT enclaves. However, the apparent advantage was somewhat misleading. Since the KMT still held the centers of power and had virtually complete control of the air, Lin Piao could not move until he was sure that KMT reinforcements would not overwhelm his rear and flanks while he conducted protracted sieges of the cities.

Except for a thin strip of territory stretching south from Changchün along the railway lines through Mukden to Chinchow in Manchuria and thence curling down to the triangle formed by Peking, Tientsin, and Paoting, the Communists controlled Manchuria and northeast China at the beginning of 1947. Their plans called for strikes from their secure base in order to divert the concerted offensives Generalissimo Chiang was conducting in the spring of 1947. Following that strategy, the Communists sacrificed Yenan, drawing substantial Nationalist forces into a campaign against a city important only as a symbol. Mao Tse-tung himself fled into the hills of north Shensi and then east to Shansi, carrying his military headquarters with him. The Nationalists thought they had won a great victory, but they had actually walked into a trap.

In July, 1947, the Communists launched their first major counterstroke. They at once enlarged their territory and drew KMT troops southward—away from Manchuria in the north, the area Mao Tse-tung, Chu Teh, and Lin Piao had chosen as the decisive battleground. A Communist Field Army under Liu Po-ch'eng, the one-eyed general, thrust through Anhwei into southern Honan Province, threatening the triplet industrial cities called Wuhan—and the Yangtze River, the traditional dividing line between north and south China. Danger to Nationalist communications intensified in August, 1947, when a Communist corps moved into western Honan, shaking the KMT's hold on all Central China. The Nationalists responded piecemeal and were defeated. Large numbers of their dispirited, unpaid, and ill-fed troops deserted in formation and under arms to the Communists.

Skirmishing continued in both Central China and
Manchuria for the better part of a year. It was punctu-
ated by political maneuvering. Chiang Kai-shek was
elected president of the Republic of China under the
constitution adopted in 1946, while Mao Tse-tung
promulgated a new law giving the land to the peasants
who tilled it. Propaganda duels continued unabated,
with the Communists generally getting the better of the
exchange. Intellectual leaders rallied to the Communists
in growing numbers.

By the summer of 1948, Lin Piao was finally ready to
move. He attacked the southern end of the strip of Manchuria which the Nationalists still held along the railroad, besieging Chinchow. Nationalist troops attempting
to lift the siege were defeated unit by unit, and Lin Piao
was on his way to victory. By the beginning of November, 1948, he had rolled up the Nationalist-held strip in
Manchuria with the fall of Mukden and Changchün. He
was ready to move against the centers of power in north
China itself, just south of the Great Wall—Peking,
Tientsin, and Paoting. But Mao Tse-tung stayed his
hand. He feared that excessive pressure would drive the
Nationalists to evacuate all their troops from the north
in order to maintain their hold on the area south of the
Yangtze River, where Communist strength was still limited to roving guerrilla bands.

Mao remembered both Chinese history and the hard-
won lessons of his guerrilla campaigns. Manchuria and
North China lay within his grasp. But he knew that several Imperial dynasties had held out "south of the
[Yangtze] River" for decades against invaders who already controlled the north. Since he wanted quick victory, rather than a protracted struggle, his main target
became the Nationalist armies. His purpose was to
demoralize and destroy the KMT forces, rather than

merely to seize real estate. He had already demonstrated his contempt for holding territory for its own sake, as less imaginative commanders were wont to do, when he casually handed Yenan over to the Nationalists. His purpose was to keep the Nationalists fighting in the north until he had broken their will by breaking their best armies.

From November, 1948, to January, 1949, he accordingly concentrated on a diversionary campaign. The city of Hsüchow in northern Kiangsu Province, just south of the Yellow River, was the focus of a fierce battle the Nationalists never should have fought. The Communist armies that had struck at Honan and Anhwei in the preceding year concentrated their attentions on Hsüchow, which fell in late December, 1948. The Nationalists had lost several hundred thousand of their best troops, and the balance of strength was tilting in the Communists' favor.

Finally in December, 1948, Mao gave the order Lin Piao had been awaiting. In conjunction with the North China Army Group of General Nieh Jung-chen, which moved west from Shantung, he began the attack on Peking, the ancient capital of China. Following Mao's orders to entrap the Nationalist forces, the combined Communist armies maneuvered to encircle government troops in the north. They also negotiated with Nationalist General Fu Tso-yi, commanding the Peking area. The Communists did not disdain the traditional Chinese weapon of bribery, called "silver bullets." Even before Fu Tso-yi, later rewarded by appointment as Minister of Water Conservancy in the People's Government, surrendered Peking at the end of January, Mao turned his forces against the remaining Nationalist troops in the area. By the end of January, 1949, all North China lay in his hands. Even more important, the government had lost

1.5 million troops in battle and through desertion between September, 1948, and January, 1949.

Continuing resistance might still have been possible militarily, but Nationalist demoralization was too great. Chiang Kai-shek had, once again, resigned as president of the Republic of China in response to criticism. Some Nationalist generals were negotiating with the Communists, and others were leading their forces in mass surrender. Many Nationalist generals found their troops deserting of their own will. Although the KMT still held vast areas of south and western China, the war was, for practical purposes, over. The government fled from Nanking to Canton, then from Canton to Chungking. The Nationalists were back where they had started five years earlier, but this time the country was against them. Once more in the president's chair, Chiang Kai-shek rejected the advice of generals who wished to repeat the long resistance to the Japanese from the wartime capital. He ordered his government to withdraw to the island of Formosa, thus ceding all of continental China to the Communists and condemning himself to exile.

Chiang Kai-shek had done a thorough job of packing his effects for exile. He took not only art treasures, his remaining loyal troops, including the Chinese Air Force, to the number of 600,000, but even Young Marshal Chang, still under house arrest. Mao Tse-tung's forces quickly rolled up the rest of China. By the end of 1949, they had occupied Szechwan in the far southwest. The country was theirs after a quarter century of struggle.

Communism had not formally come to China, but only the transitional stage Mao called the New Democracy. A conference of 561 delegates handpicked by the Communists met in Peking in September, 1949, to lacquer the facade of the "coalition government of all demo-

cratic elements" the Communists were erecting. The
Chinese People's Political Consultative Council duti-
fully carried out its assigned tasks. Hardly pausing for
breath, it "enacted" a series of statutes. Chief among
them were: the Organic Law (Provisional Constitution)
of the Central People's Government of the People's Republic of China and the Common Program of the People's Political Consultative Conference, a statement
of the new government's intentions. The Conference
elected Mao Tse-tung Chairman (President) of the
Chinese People's Republic, adopted a new national
anthem, and proclaimed a new national flag. The red
banner with five gold stars in the upper right-hand corner representing the chief races of China was to fly over
the country thereafter. Significantly, the central star,
standing for the dominant Han—Chinese—race, was
much larger than the others, though the flag was intended to display the unity in equality of all the races of
China.

The battle for the soil of China was over, but, as soon
became apparent, the battle for the soul of China was
just beginning. The same independence, stubbornness,
and yearning for justice on the part of the Chinese people which gave the Communists control were to prevent
their peacefully ruling China by authoritarian methods
they soon adopted. The Communists had little choice of
methods, they felt. After all, their political handbooks
laid down no means of rule other than suppression and
force. Once in power, they displayed even less tolerance
of dissenters than had the Nationalists.

The Communists' foreign policy was, initially at least,
based upon a firm alliance with the Soviet Union and
great hostility to the United States. Although friendship
with the U.S.S.R. was to collapse after a decade, antago-

nism toward the U.S.A. endured for two decades. Among the first acts of the Communist government was the expulsion of almost all foreigners. Frightened by the United Nations' armies advancing up the Korean Peninsula toward Manchuria, the Chinese entered the Korean war in the fall of 1950. Chances of a reconciliation with the United States, which had been moving toward recognition of the new regime, were thus postponed—indefinitely, it appeared at that time.

In its internal aspect, Communist rule can conveniently be divided into four periods. The first lasted eight years, from 1949 to 1957; the succeeding three periods each occupied roughly three years: 1958-1960; 1961-1964; and late 1965 to early 1969. The latest period, which began enfolding in mid-1969, appeared to have re-created much of the confusion of purpose and weakness of administration against which the Communists began crusading in the warlord days.

From 1949 to 1957, Communist rule, by and large, went smoothly. Borne up by popular support and sustained by the internal stability they created and enforced, the Communists radically improved the lot of the common people. They were assisted not only by the existence of the first effective central government China had known since the early 1800s, but also by the great number of economic projects half-begun under Nationalist rule, only to be abandoned under the stress of foreign and civil war. Whatever the advantages created by circumstances, the Communists' own great diligence, efficiency, and honesty were decisive to their success during the early years. China, it appeared, finally possessed a government which really cared about the common people—and actually kept its promises.

The Communists vigorously pressed their campaign to remake China. Domestically, they strove to create a wholly altered society with a stable economic foundation. Having seized power in order to restore China's greatness, they worked strenuously abroad to make their country once again a great power.

Their first purpose was, however, to consolidate their rule by destroying their domestic enemies. Land was distributed to the poor share-croppers—and millions of landlords were executed. Private enterprise was gradually eroded by a series of "campaigns," the "great popular movements" the Communists forced upon a nation which would have preferred peace and prosperity. In 1955, the farmers, delighting in their new land, were informed that they would work more efficiently in "cooperatives," which would, in time, become "collectives," where all labored for the common good and no one for his selfish, personal interest.

The farmers were not happy. Nor were the intellectuals, who had hailed the Communist victory. In 1957, alarmed by hidden resistance and the people's passiveness, Mao Tse-tung permitted a period of free speech, under the slogan: "Let a hundred flowers blossom! Let all opinions be expressed!" He was shocked to discover that the articulate intellectuals bitterly denounced the new dictatorship he was imposing—as did non-Communist members of the "coalition government." Those ministers revealed that they exercised no real power, but were manipulated by their Communist "deputies." Mao therefore, abruptly closed the free forum he had opened. A new era of repression and purges began with the discarding of the facade of coalition government.

The year 1958 was marked by proclamation of the Great Leap Forward and the Great People's Communes. Having broken with the Soviet Union, which refused to make China a nuclear power, the Communists were determined to build an industrial base and create a "wholly new society" in a historical instant. Under the slogan "Surpass Britain in five years—and the United States in twenty years!" they drove the people to work 14- to 16-hour days on much reduced rations. The miracle of creating an industrial base in a few years' time was to be accomplished by first working another miracle: transforming the "selfish" character of human beings. The Great People's Communes abolished private property and even private homes, planning to segregate men and women in separate dormitories, while children would be raised by the benevolent State itself. The Great Leap Forward promised to increase agricultural and industrial production manyfold in a few years by the massed labor of hundreds of millions of Chinese. "People's war," that is, guerrilla struggles and subversion supported by propaganda, was to extend Chinese influence abroad—and "liberate all the oppressed of mankind." China would become a great power by unconventional means, just as the Communists had conquered China by unconventional means.

By 1960, the catastrophic failure of internal plans had produced intense resentment and disillusionment, not only among the common people, but even among senior leaders of the CCP itself. Hard-headed generals warned that "people's war" invited attack on a vulnerable China by the United States, while the quarrel with the U.S.S.R. created a grave military danger on the northern frontiers. Mao had been forced to resign as chairman of the People's Government, while remaining chairman of the CCP. He had retained the latter post only by threatening to raise a new popular rebellion against the practical men led by Marshal P'eng Teh-huai. Although P'eng was dismissed from his post as Minister of Defense and replaced by Marshal Lin Piao, a group headed by the new chairman (president) of the People's Republic, Liu

Shao-ch'i, took over. The practical men patiently began repairing the damage done by Mao's uncontrolled enthusiasm. By mid-1965, the Chinese people once more had enough to eat, a sufficiency of clothing, and were living in normal households. The Great Leap Forward and the Great People's Communes were still praised in slogans, but were ignored in reality. The hard-line Maoists cried out that China was moving away from—rather than towards—Communism.

In 1966, the hard-line Maoists initiated one of history's more astonishing political movements. They deliberately set out to destroy both the Communist Party and the Central People's Government, because, they said, both had been overrun by "capitalist agents, headed by Liu Shao-ch'i." Mao Tse-tung incited the "people's rebellion" he had earlier threatened. For three years, the battle surged back and forth. In the beginning, the Red Guards, youths and girls—angry at the Communist bureaucrats and organized by the Maoists—rampaged across China. They had been ordered by Mao Tse-tung and Lin Piao: "Make rebellion and destroy the old civilization!" Disorder became acute when workers and peasants, backed by intellectuals and old officials of the CCP, resisted the Red Guards. In February, 1967, the People's Liberation Army was instructed to "end anarchy," maintain order, and "seize power" for the Maoists.

For the first time, Communist troops were used against the common people—and against the Communist Party itself. By a natural process, the Liberation Army began taking real control of the country. All the men who held power still shouted slogans glorifying Mao Tse-tung, but they followed their own policies, which usually ran counter to Mao's. Nonetheless, disorder continued to spread. Neither the leadership in Peking nor the Revolutionary Committees, the new governments in the provinces, could agree among themselves on policies—or personalities. Purge followed purge, with the military's power growing ever greater.

The eclipse of central power inevitably shifted remaining power to the provinces. Communist generals survived and expanded their authority because of the number of troops under their command and the extent of the areas they controlled. China did not return totally to the era of the warlords, for the central government in Peking still possessed adherents throughout the country. But regional authority, based upon military force, was the chief political force in the nation. "Power," as Mao had observed, "grows from the barrel of the gun!"

When the Chinese Communist Party held its Ninth National Congress in Peking in April, 1969, the Chinese leaders felt revulsion against violence and disorder. The new, predominantly military leadership sought to placate the people by promising that terror would end. A new, more conciliatory foreign policy was also tentatively set in motion. But the Chinese people had taken all they would. Besides, the men in the provinces enjoyed their new power. Even if they had not, no really effective central authority existed. Still, Mao Tse-tung proclaimed his policy of "continuing revolution." It required no feat of memory to recall Dr. Sun Yat-sen's deathbed injunction: "The revolution is not yet completed!"

Instead of ending strife, the Communists had created a new era of strife. Something was seriously wrong with the "inevitable historical process" described by Marxism. The normal cycle of Chinese history was also out of phase. Apparently the time had not yet come for a stable dynasty to impose order—as stable dynasties had always followed periods of disorder through 2,000 years of Imperial history. Having taken power by deceit and the sword, the Communists were in danger of perishing by deceit and the sword.

The Biblical allusion may be unfairly applied to a Far Eastern country. To refer to a more modern source, the dying Maoist era had demonstrated the truth of the political maxim based upon Isaac Newton's third law of motion: "Any action creates a counter-action of equal force."

The Maoists had clearly demonstrated that violence generates counter-violence of equal force. The Maoists had shown that the Chinese people could be led but could not be driven beyond a certain point. Revolution produced counter-revolution of equal force—for the Communists had always used much force.

Once again at the end of the 1960s, the future of China seemed obscure, as obscure as it had been when Sun Yat-Sen lay dying in Peking in March of 1925. But a new phase had already begun. It was the most hopeful phase of modern Chinese history since Sun Yat-sen's Revolution of 1911 had destroyed the decayed Empire. Mao Tse-tung had failed to make China the Marxist earthly paradise of which he dreamed by the harsh measures he favored. He had, further, failed to make China a great conventional power, though the People's Republic possessed nuclear arms and was a force that could not be ignored.

Because of his failures and his advanced age—79 in 1972—he was reduced to a figurehead. Men still swore loudly that they followed his teachings, but practical policy was made by more realistic officials and generals gathered around Premier Chou En-lai, himself 74 in 1972. Those "moderates" sought to reach attainable goals, rather than pursuing impossible dreams of creating

Utopia at home and liberation, which meant concealed conquest, abroad.

China was primarily ruled by generals, though large areas were not wholly receptive to Peking's orders. Those generals strove for order and better living conditions within China, while seeking to make China secure against attack from without. They did not seek to fulfill Mao's visions of a "perfect, new Communist society."

One of the first—and most spectacular—results of the new political line was President Richard M. Nixon's visit to China in February, 1972. Once again, after a lapse of two decades, the United States was resuming contact with China.

Both countries appeared to have learned much. The Chinese had, it seemed, learned that they could neither accomplish the impossible at home nor dominate the world abroad. The United States, it seemed, had learned that it could not control events in China, but must live amicably with a great nation determined to go its own way. With new maturity on both sides, the prospects seemed good.

Ironically, Chiang Kai-shek in exile on Formosa, and Mao Tse-tung isolated in Peking, were no longer the figures determining the fate of the nation. Their intense, personal battle, fought for almost four decades, had ended in a virtual draw. New men were making new policies for a new world.

Index

About the Author

Robert S. Elegant, a native New Yorker, has returned to Hong Kong, where he was chief of bureau for the *Los Angeles Times* from 1965 to 1970. In the interim, he was based in Munich, Germany, as foreign affairs columnist for the *Times* and the *Los Angeles Times/Washington Post News Service*, serving 350 newspapers. A University of Pennsylvania graduate (Phi Beta Kappa), he also attended Yale's Institute of Far Eastern Language and Literature. He holds an M.A. in Chinese and Japanese and an M.S. in Journalism from Columbia.

He served in the U.S. Army from 1946 to 1948 and has been a foreign correspondent since 1951, having received fellowships from the Pulitzer and Ford Foundations during the period. In the last twenty-one years, his work as a journalist has led him to residence in Korea, Japan, India, Singapore, Hong Kong, Spain, and Germany. Mr. Elegant has traveled throughout the world and has received numerous prizes for his work, including three Annual Awards from the Overseas Press Club for Best Interpretation of Foreign News, an honor he shares with only one other, Walter Lippmann. He has lectured widely and written numerous magazine articles and is the author of four other important non-fiction works on Asia, as well as two novels.

He was married in New Delhi, India, in 1956 to Moira Clarissa Brady of Sidney, Australia, and is the father of two children, Victoria Ann and Simon David Brady, who assisted greatly in the preparation of this book.